JOHN DEWEY IN CHINA

SUNY series in Chinese Philosophy and Culture
Roger T. Ames, editor

JOHN DEWEY
IN CHINA

To Teach and to Learn

Jessica Ching-Sze Wang

STATE UNIVERSITY OF NEW YORK PRESS

Photo of John Dewey and Alice Chipman Dewey with Hu Shih and
Tao Xingzhi in Nanjing, China (1920), used with the permission of
Special Collections Research Center, Morris Library, Southern Illinois
University at Carbondale, U.S.A.

Published by

State University of New York Press, Albany

© 2007 State University of New York

For information, contact
State University of New York Press,
www.sunypress.edu, Albany, NY

Production by Marilyn P. Semerad
Marketing by Michael Campochiaro

Library of Congress Cataloging-in-Publication Data

Wang, Jessica Ching-Sze.
    John Dewey in China : to teach and to learn / Jessica Ching-Sze Wang.
        p. cm. — (Suny series in Chinese philosophy and culture)
    Includes bibliographical references and index.
    ISBN 978-0-7914-7203-3 (hardcover : alk. paper)
    ISBN 978-0-7914-7204-0 (pbk. : alk. paper)
    1. Dewey, John, 1859–1952. 2. Social sciences—Philosophy. 3. Education—Philosophy.
4. Political science—Philosophy. 5. United States—Foreign relations—China. 6. China—
Foreign relations—United States. I. Title.
B945.D44C44 2007
191—dc22   2006036597

10 9 8 7 6 5 4 3 2 1

CONTENTS

———❖———

ACKNOWLEDGMENTS

———❖———

My study on John Dewey's visit to China could not have been possible without the assistance and support of many individuals. First, I would like to thank Dr. Roger Ames and Dr. Jim Tiles for introducing me to this important topic and for offering constructive feedback throughout the years. I am especially indebted to Dr. Ames for encouraging me to convert my dissertation into a book and recommending my work to the State University of New York Press.

My greatest debt is to Dr. Barry Bull, my dissertation advisor. His guidance has been a tremendous help in developing my ideas. I especially appreciated his editorial suggestions on the various drafts. His strong sense of duty as an academic is exemplary. I also want to thank the other members of my dissertation committee, Dr. Luise McCarty, Dr. Jeff Wasserstrom, and Dr. Don Warren. I am particularly grateful to Dr. McCarty, whose constant warmth and support made my life as a graduate student a very enjoyable and rewarding experience. I am also very fortunate to have met Dr. Wasserstrom, whose scholarly expertise and personal generosity have contributed greatly to the development of my research.

My work has also benefited substantially from informal conversations with other scholars. Special thanks to Dr. Heidi Ross for inspiring the subtitle of my book, to Dr. David Wong for acknowledging the contribution of my work, to Dr. Vera Schwarcz for sharing her insights about May Fourth China, and above all, to Dr. Jim Garrison for sharpening my understanding about John Dewey. I also want to thank my two readers at SUNY Press. Their thoughtful comments helped improve the revision of the manuscript. In addition, my conversations with Dr. Larry Hickman and Dr. Matthew Pamental were very helpful for the revision. The content of the final printed book, however, is my own responsibility.

I would like to acknowledge the assistance of several institutions that have made the completion of my work possible. First, I am grateful to the East–West Center for sponsoring my two-year study at the University of Hawaii and for making my dream to study in the United States come true. I would also like to express my deepest gratitude to the School of Education at Indiana University, Bloomington, for providing a four-year Chancellor's fellowship that enabled me to complete my graduate studies without financial worries, and to the Chiang Ching-kuo Foundation for its dissertation fellowship that allowed me to concentrate on writing for one year. I am also thankful to the Center for Dewey Studies at Southern Illinois University for assisting me with the collection of materials. Finally, I am grateful to my colleges and students at the National Chiayi University in Taiwan for providing a friendly and comfortable work environment that helped me complete the manuscript. In addition, I would like to thank Purdue University Press for granting me permission to reprint the following material in chapter four: Jessica Ching-Sze Wang, "John Dewey as a Learner in China," in *E&C/Education and Culture* 21 (1) (2005): 59–73.

My acknowledgments would not be complete without mentioning those who are close to me. I want to thank my parents, my husband, Hsiao-tzu Yang, and my best friend, Meichun, for their unyielding love and support. I also want to express gratitude to the following people who assisted me in various ways during the revision of the manuscript: my friends, Vincent and Mira, and my teaching assistant, Suechin. I also have to thank my best teachers, Ms. Deborah Brody in particular, for making a difference in my life. Finally, I am indebted to John Dewey for living out his own philosophy. I dedicate this book to him.

CHAPTER 1

DEWEY AND MAY FOURTH CHINA

Enacting a Historical Drama

The American philosopher John Dewey visited China in May 1919 and departed in July 1921. Coinciding with the well-known May Fourth movement, Dewey's two-year visit demarcated a significant episode in the history of intellectual exchange between China and the United States. In a narrow sense, the May Fourth movement refers to the student demonstration in Beijing on May 4, 1919, in protest of the Versailles Peace Conference. In a broader sense, it represented a vast modernization movement from 1917 through 1921, which sought to reform China through intellectual and social means.[1] Interestingly, history creates its own dramas. Had the movement not occurred in May 1919, Dewey might not have lingered in China for two years and two months. To understand the significance of Dewey's encounter with May Fourth China—where it all began and how it unfolded—we need to place his visit in a larger historical context, namely, the history of contact between China and the modern West.

China began to enter truly into the Western consciousness in the sixteenth century as a land of tea and a potential kingdom of God. At the beginning of their contact, the West was a learner as well as a suppliant. It attempted to seek close relations with China to advance its trade and enrich its culture.[2] Nevertheless, China long remained indifferent to Western influence. In 1793 a British ambassador arrived in China to establish formal diplomatic relations and open more sea ports for trade. However, in his letter to British King George III, the Ching Emperor Qianlong stated, "we have never valued ingenious articles, nor do we have the

1

slightest need of your country's manufactures." He wrote to the British king, "Simply act in conformity with our wishes by strengthening your loyalty and swearing perpetual obedience so as to ensure that your country may share the blessings of peace."[3]

Ironically, peace was not to follow from the emperor's complacent, isolationist stance in the face of increasing aggression on the part of foreign traders and diplomats. The glorious past of Chinese civilization was soon to pale before the technological advancement of the West. Beginning in the mid-nineteenth century, China faced a series of military defeats, starting with the first Opium War with Great Britain (1839–1842), continuing with the second Opium War with Great Britain and France (1856–1860), and culminating in the most humiliating of all, the Sino-Japanese War (1894–1895), in which China fell at the hands of a neighbor who for centuries had paid tribute to the imperial court of China and revered her as a cultural model. These devastating defeats led to the signing of an array of unequal treaties that forced China to concede many of her territorial and sovereignty rights. Barely a century after the Qianlong emperor's edict, the young Guangxu emperor issued a new imperial statement in 1898, acknowledging that "the methods of government inaugurated by Sung and Ming dynasties, upon investigation, reveal nothing of any practical use. . . . Changes must be made to accord with the necessities of times."[4] The transformation of China's attitude toward the West was most evident in the 1901 edict in which the Empress Dowager was reported to have recognized "the necessity of appropriating the good qualities of foreign nations" so that "the shortcomings of China may be supplemented, and that the experiences of the past may serve a lesson for the future."[5]

The Opium War with Great Britain marked a turning point in the history of contact between China and the West. Before the war, the exchange had always been on China's terms, but after the war, it was on the West's terms. Antiforeign feelings naturally arose. In 1900 the Boxer Uprising erupted, starting as a peasant uprising in Shandong that aimed to drive foreigners out of China. The so-called boxers practiced martial arts and believed that certain talismans would protect them from foreign firearms. The movement gradually spread to Beijing, where the boxers, encouraged by Empress Dowager, began to burn down churches and foreign residences and to kill Chinese Christians and Western missionaries. Finally, internationally organized troops wrested control of Beijing from the boxers and released all hostages, thus putting an end to this violent and disastrous confrontation between Chinese and foreigners.[6] The Boxer Uprising resulted not only in the imperial court's reform but also in a settlement that required China to pay a huge indemnity to Russia, Germany, France, Great Britain, and the United States. Nonetheless, at this low point in Sino-Western relations, Western powers did not have a uniform approach to China. During the Boxer crisis, they reacted "with varying degrees of sternness toward the Chinese."[7] The U.S. government was sympathetic to the Chinese while attempting to protect its own interests. A few years after the signing of the final settlement, the U.S. government returned a large portion of its share of the indemnity payments—on the condition that the money should be used to fund scholarships for study in the United States.

One of the most important episodes in the history of intellectual exchange between China and the United States was to grow out of this effort of the U.S. government to promote the education of China's young elites. Hu Shih, Dewey's chief disciple in China, received a scholarship from the indemnity funds to study in the United States in 1910. Had it not been for the scholarship, Hu could not have studied at Columbia under the tutelage of Dewey.[8] Had it not been for Hu's close acquaintance with Dewey, Dewey could not have been the first foreign scholar to be formally invited to lecture in China in 1919. Nonetheless, we have so far answered only half of a puzzle about Dewey's encounter with China, namely, what brought Hu Shih to Dewey. The other half of the puzzle concerns what initially brought Dewey to the Far East.

In the fall of 1918, Dewey was on a sabbatical leave from Columbia University and was teaching at the University of California at Berkeley. Because Dewey and his wife, Alice, were geographically nearer to Asia than they would otherwise have been, they thought they might as well take this opportunity and travel to Japan in the spring. Dewey also agreed to this plan because this trip might help cure Alice's longtime depression over the death of their son on a trip to Italy.[9] When two of Dewey's Japanese acquaintances learned that he was planning a trip to Japan, they arranged for him to deliver a series of lectures at Tokyo Imperial University. When Hu Shih and other former students of Dewey at Columbia University learned of Dewey's visit to Japan, they tried to contact him there and invited him to spend a year in China as a visiting scholar. Dewey was very glad to receive their invitation. He entertained the idea of visiting China in the summer before returning to the United States, but he did not know how long he could stay. Columbia University might not grant him a leave of absence for a full year. However, this seemed like an attractive plan to Dewey because he thought, "In a year one could begin to learn something of the East."[10] Even though Dewey received the notification from Columbia on April 15 that his leave of absence was approved, he did not promise to stay a year in China until he arrived there in person. He needed to evaluate the prospects in China to make an informed decision.

This was not an easy decision. Dewey told his children, "Every other day I have cold feet about the whole proposition" because many people

warned him about making contract with the Chinese.[11] Dewey had financial concerns because he "had always been close to being poor."[12] In fact,
he could not have afforded the trip to Japan if his close friend, Albert C.
Barnes, had not offered financial support. Barnes proposed to pay Dewey
a monthly stipend on the condition Dewey "make a report on Japan as
a factor in the future international relation."[13] Apart from financial inse-
curity, Dewey was also concerned about the program his disciples were
arranging for him. In a letter to his son, Dewey wrote:

> My former Chinese students seem to be making as elaborate plans
> for our reception as we have enjoyed here. The only trouble is that
> I shall have to lecture all the time to help even up. I don't know the
> program exactly, but I know it calls for lectures in Shanghai, Nanking
> and Peking and I assume other places. You look up your geography
> and you will see how far apart the places are.[14]

Although Dewey had mixed feelings about the proposed plan of his
one-year visit in China, Hu Shih was busy laying the groundwork for
his reception.

On May 1, 1919, Dewey expressed excitement upon arrival in China.
"We are going to see more of the dangerous daring side of life here I pre-
dict," he wrote. "We are very obviously in the hands of young China. What
it will do with us makes us laugh to anticipate." He added, "Nothing wor-
ries us. . . . We ought to have a very good time. Quite unlike anything in
Japan."[15] For Dewey, Japan seemed like "a land of reserves and reticence"
(MW 11: 174).[16] He was delighted to find that the social atmosphere in
China was much more open and free flowing. The significant differences
Dewey perceived between Japan and China led him to remark, "every
American who goes to Japan ought also to visit China—if only to com-
plete his education" (MW 11: 179). Dewey was right about the "dangerous
daring side of life" in China. Three days after he made this remark, Dewey
learned of a serious student revolt that broke out in Beijing.

On May 4, 1919, from which the May Fourth movement took its name,
more than 3,000 students in Beijing held a mass demonstration against
the decision of the Versailles Peace Conference to transfer German conces-
sions in Shantung to Japan. With their dream of world peace shattered by
this unjust decision, the students were mortified and outraged. To protest
against Japanese imperialism and government corruption, they took to
the streets, burned the house of one corrupt, pro-Japanese official, and
physically assaulted another. The students' expression of patriotism and
zeal for reform triggered similar demonstrations throughout China in the
few weeks that followed. Several students were killed in these incidents,
and many were arrested. In big cities, people went on general strikes to

support the students and promoted boycotts against Japanese goods. Seeing that public opinion was on the side of the students, the government agreed to release those who were jailed. Nevertheless, this was not enough to appease the students. They refused to leave the jail unless the government agreed to dismiss corrupt officials, reject the signing of the Versailles peace treaty, and allow freedom of speech at public gatherings.

Dewey's response to the May Fourth movement was more than enthusiastic; the social energies being released galvanized him. As Dewey wrote to his children in June 1919, "never in our lives had we begun to learn as much as in the last four months. And the last month particularly, there has been too much food to be digestible."[17] Indeed, the May Fourth movement was China's gift to Dewey. It kept him excited, involved, puzzled, and, at times, frustrated. It was also intellectual bait that enticed Dewey to stay in China for a full year, and later, to extend his stay for a second year. Dewey said, "To the outward eye roaming in search of the romantic and picturesque, China is likely to prove a disappointment. To the eye of the mind it presents the most enthralling drama now anywhere enacting" (MW 11: 215). On the Chinese stage, Dewey was both a spectator and a player. His roles were multiple, depending on who was directing, watching, and judging. However, the existing literature fails to capture the full story of Dewey's visit in China.

Rethinking Dewey's Visit in China

The 1920s demarcates an important period in the life of John Dewey: his trips to Japan, China, Russia, Mexico, and Turkey undoubtedly broadened his horizon and enriched his understanding of world cultures. Of all the foreign countries Dewey visited, China is where he stayed the longest and about which he wrote the most extensively. However, this particular phase in the life and work of Dewey has been largely ignored and, even when taken seriously, misunderstood. Compared to the huge bulk of literature on Dewey and his voluminous works, studies on Dewey's encounter with China are meager. Only two major books have been published, and only one issue has been raised and studied, namely, how Dewey influenced China.

The first book was published in 1973, *Lectures in China, 1919–1920*. It originated from a research project of the East–West Center to translate Dewey's lectures into English. In their introduction to the book, Clopton and Ou assert that Dewey's influence on Chinese education was "profound and extensive."[18] According to Ou, "[n]o dissenting views were ever voiced during the time of Dewey's visit nor for many years afterwards. Dewey became the highest educational authority in China."[19] The second book, Barry Keenan's *The Dewey Experiment in China*, was published in 1977. Keenan claims that "Deweyan experimentalism, as a way of thinking, as a way of acting politically, and as a component of democratic education, offered no strategies his followers could use to affect political power."[20] Owing to a serious lack of subsequent research, Keenan's book has been regarded as the single most authoritative account of Dewey's visit in China.

However, the conclusions of these early works—that Dewey contributed greatly to the modernization of Chinese education but failed to influence political change in China—are seriously problematic. Ou's claim about Dewey's influence on Chinese education, if not entirely inadequate, is simplistic at best because it is primarily based on the evidence of external institutional changes. According to Suzanne Pepper, the Chinese school system from 1900 to 1937 was in constant flux; China's education reform was characterized by a superficial copying of foreign educational systems—first Japanese, then American, and French.[21] No data are available to ascertain how these policy changes affected actual classroom practices.

Although a pioneering historical study, Keenan's book provides only superficial treatment of Dewey. He focuses largely on the frustrated attempts of Dewey's disciples to apply his ideas to the reform of China, while treating Dewey and his philosophy as distant background. Keenan fails to do justice to Dewey as a philosopher by ignoring his unique perspective on what was happening to and around him. Above all, the assumption about "the Dewey experiment"—that his visit was intended to bring about dramatic change—makes Dewey an easy target. It is not fair to expect a foreign philosopher to resolve the social and political problems of China. Although Keenan's underlying portrait of Dewey as a savior may have captured the wishful thinking of many Chinese at that time, it was inconsistent with Dewey's character and his own intentions. Dewey would not want his ideas to be simply accepted and copied. In "Transforming the Mind of China," written in late 1919, Dewey clearly stated that China's development toward democracy "must be a transforming growth from within, rather than either an external superimposition or a borrowing from foreign sources" (MW 11: 213). In a letter he wrote to a colleague at Columbia University, Dewey perceived his "influence" as nothing more than "a sort of outside reinforcement . . . to the young or liberal element . . . in spite of its vagueness."[22]

Nonetheless, under the influence of these early studies, Dewey scholars today have serious misconceptions about his visit to China. In his influential book, *John Dewey and American Democracy* (1991), Robert Westbrook cites Keenan's critique of Dewey and comments that "Chinese Deweyans suffered from the same strategic weakness as Dewey's own hopes to make the school the unsteepled church of democracy."[23] In *John*

Dewey and the High Tide of American Liberalism (1995), Alan Ryan accepts the view about Dewey's immense popularity in China and attributes it to the inherent commonalities between Dewey's vision of democracy and "Confucian ideals of family and community loyalty."[24] Ryan's explanation is problematic in that he fails to consider that the May Fourth movement was noted for its antitraditionalism. In fact, Dewey was well received because he was thought to represent an alternative to Confucianism. Ryan also assumes the similarities between Dewey and Confucius to be the reason why Dewey was more popular than Bertrand Russell, who was also visiting China at that time. However, the assumption about Dewey's greater popularity remains to be examined.

A survey of the existing literature leaves one with the impression that no interesting issues beyond the extent of Dewey's influence on China are worth examining. The important question of what Dewey was experiencing, thinking, and learning while he was in China has not been addressed. According to Dewey's own daughter, his time in China "had a deep and enduring influence upon him."[25] No matter what influence Dewey may have had on China, this visit was a vital part of his own education. As Dewey himself wrote in a letter, "I prize highly the unusual opportunity to get some acquaintance with Oriental thought and conditions."[26] In one article Dewey stated, "Simply as an intellectual spectacle, a scene for study and surmise, for investigation and speculation, there is nothing in the world today—not even Europe in the throes of reconstruction—that equals China. History records no parallel" (MW 13: 94). The intellectual interest China presented to Dewey was indeed phenomenal. However, neither Keenan's book nor subsequent studies address Dewey's own learning in China. In his recent biography of Dewey, *The Education of John Dewey* (2002), Jay Martin writes that Dewey "had become a changed person, or more precisely, an evolving person" after his visit to China, but Martin does not elaborate specifically on how Dewey was changed.[27] We now need to ask the question of how China may have influenced Dewey rather than how Dewey influenced China.

My book attempts to answer several important questions that have remained largely unexamined. For instance, how was Dewey received and understood by the Chinese? What were Dewey's own thoughts and reflections on his experiences in China? How did the visit relate to the larger context of his life and work? How did it affect the subsequent development of Dewey's philosophy? The testimony of Dewey's Chinese disciples and supporters have greatly influenced current scholarly opinion. A study of archival documents in China reveals that left-wing radicals and right-wing traditionalists received Dewey's ideas critically. To explore Dewey's learning experiences in China, we need to look into the letters Dewey exchanged with his children, colleagues, and friends during his stay. We also need to examine some forty articles Dewey wrote for the *New Republic* and *Asia,* which Walter Lippmann praised as "models of what political reporting ought to be."[28] Alan Ryan was wrong to assume that these articles merely dealt with "momentarily important issues that now interest only the historians of international relations."[29] A close reading of these articles, in conjunction with a careful study of Dewey's political writings, shows that his visit to China had a significant impact on the development of his social and political philosophy.

My book draws heavily on historical materials that have been made available through a research trip to China and through the publication of Dewey's lifetime correspondence. These materials do not simply add to the pool of evidence already available; they allow us to reread formerly available materials from new perspectives. They enable us to unravel the complexities and volatilities of Dewey's reception in China and the richness of his own experiences. In short, these materials help deepen our understanding of Dewey's encounter with China, especially where it concerns his reception by the general public, his own learning, and its impact on his philosophy.

The Encounter between Dewey and China: Then and Now

The encounter between Dewey and China in the 1920s was characterized by ambivalences, uncertainties, and changes on both sides. Faced with challenges from the West, Chinese intellectuals had initially sought to acquire Western technology and implement Western institutions. Later, they realized that they had to study the ideas that inform Western development and practice. This meant that Chinese intellectual tradition could no longer remain intact and unimpaired. On the basis of this realization, the May Fourth intelligentsia savagely attacked their Confucian tradition. Early opposition to this antitraditionalist, iconoclastic trend was feeble. However, toward the end of the May Fourth period, especially after 1921, traditionalist sentiments, fermented by nationalistic feelings, were beginning to gain momentum.[30] Dewey correctly characterized the intellectual landscape as vexed by "confusion, uncertainty, mutual criticism and hostility among the various tendencies." During the two years of his stay, Dewey came into contact with these contending ideologies that made Young China an "ambiguous" term, signifying "all kinds of contradictory aspirations" (MW 13: 112). Examining the reception of Dewey's ideas in China will show how these uncertainties and contradictions among Chinese intellectuals affected their views of Dewey.

Although Chinese intellectuals had ambivalent attitudes toward the West, Dewey had his doubts about how the United States should respond to China, or rather, how the United States could help China.

As demonstrated herein, Dewey was trying to understand China and its precarious position in the international world, while Chinese intellectuals were trying to understand Dewey and his position in their ideological battles. Dewey was eventually able to understand China on its own terms and to propose thoughtful suggestions concerning the United States' responsibility to China. On the other hand, many Chinese created images of Dewey on their own terms to meet their own needs. Changes in Dewey's views about China resulted from his own learning and reflection, whereas shifting views of Dewey among Chinese intellectuals reflected their deep-seated frustrations with contemporary events that led either to increasing radicalism or to conservatism.

The dialogue between Dewey and China has been ongoing and tends to be shaped by the historical circumstances and dominant ideologies of each era. In the 1920s, Chinese opinions of Dewey reflected their own vexed interests in liberalism, neotraditionalism, and Marxism. In the 1930s and 1940s, as China underwent a series of domestic and international wars, a natural eclipse of interest in Dewey occurred. Since the establishment of the Communist regime in 1949, the dialogue between Dewey and China took a drastic turn. In the 1950s and 1960s, the Chinese Communist government launched a large-scale campaign to purge the pragmatic influences of Hu Shih and Dewey. During this period, pragmatism was eschewed as an evil influence of Western imperialism and capitalism. In the 1980s, due to the Reform and Open Door policy of China, the dialogue about Dewey was revived.[31] Since then, Chinese scholars have started to reevaluate Dewey and pragmatism.[32] In fact, between 1999 and 2001, three collections of Dewey's lectures in China were reprinted. At the turn of the twenty-first century, China is ready to review and rethink her past. Before we applaud the resurgence of scholarly interest in Dewey and his influence on Chinese philosophy and modern education, we need to return to the original encounter in the 1920s and explore the unique story of Dewey's visit from his own perspective as a teacher and a learner.

Overview of Upcoming Chapters

The chapters that follow present a combination of biography and philosophy to correct misrepresentations of Dewey in the existing literature and to cast a new light on his philosophy. Although my study draws on the intellectual and political history of China, particularly during the May Fourth era, I do not wish to suggest that it is a complete account of that period. I offer my interpretations as an attempt to understand what happened to Dewey in China. Therefore, I focus on the views of Dewey and those directly or indirectly associated with him.

Chapter two examines Dewey's role as a teacher during his visit, focusing on what Dewey said to the Chinese, what kind of teacher he was, and how he compared to Bertrand Russell. The contents of Dewey's lectures are examined in relation to the particular images associated with him, such as "Mr. Science," "Mr. Democracy," and as the common people's educator. Dewey is then examined as a benevolent and democratic teacher. In addition, I discuss the problem of translation in Dewey's lectures, asking whether the Chinese texts of Dewey's lectures were unequivocal representations of what he said. Possible discrepancies in Hu Shih's translation point to the danger of evaluating Dewey based solely on these lectures without looking into his own writings in English. Moreover, I explore important differences between Dewey and his chief disciple and Chinese translator, Hu Shih. Hu's cultural and intellectualistic approach to reform diverged from Dewey's more practical and pragmatic stance. Hu's proposal for full-scale Westernization also runs a sharp contrast to Dewey's advice for China. Dewey hoped that China would not imitate the West blindly but would rely on its own cultural strengths to transform itself from within. Having differentiated Dewey from Hu, I contend that one should not hold Dewey accountable for Hu's reform ideas. Instead, one should seek to discover and evaluate Dewey's ideas in their own right. In addition, I discuss the controversial question of whether Hu Shih was a true pragmatist and whether his "pragmatist experiment" in China could offer us some insights about the challenges for pragmatism in the global context.

Chapter three looks at the reception of Dewey's ideas in China. First, I present a chronological account of Dewey's reception during his stay, focusing on the enthusiasm on his arrival, followed by a slight decline in mid-1920 owing to Russell's rivalry and an increasing radicalism among Chinese intellectuals. Then I continue to examine critical responses to Dewey after his departure, focusing on the reception of Dewey's social and political thought and educational theories. Socialists and Marxists challenged Dewey's social and political philosophy, whereas traditionalists criticized his educational ideas. Some of the criticisms were ideological accusations, whereas others result from underlying differences in cultural beliefs and practices. The chapter concludes by returning to the theme of "the Dewey Experiment in China." In one sense, the experiment really existed, granted that a wide range of Chinese intellectuals experimented with Dewey as a symbol of their own conflicting desires. Dewey was co-opted by liberals, traditionalists and socialists alike, all using him to validate their own ideas or to attack their enemies. As a result, Dewey meant different things to different people. Finally, I present my own rendering of the Dewey experiment—one that Dewey himself was conducting. Determined to understand China on its own terms, the U.S. philosopher undertook himself to dissect the problem of Eurocentrism.

Chapter four looks at Dewey as a learner, featuring his role as a political commentator, a goodwill ambassador, and a cultural anthropologist. I discuss Dewey's evolving views about the May Fourth movement, the responsibility of the United States in the Far East, and Chinese ways of life. Dewey wrote thoughtfully and insightfully about China. His intellectual curiosity and open-mindedness were exemplary for those interested in intercultural understanding. In his long sojourn, Dewey came to understand Chinese social and political psychology and philosophy of life. At the same time, he also learned about the West—its Eurocentric worldviews, its secret diplomacy, and its sense of superiority as an international political and cultural force. Finally, I discuss the meanings of Dewey's journey in the larger context of his personal life and work.

Chapter five contends that Dewey's learning in China contributed to his evolving thought about internationalism, the relations between the public and the state, and most important, about the distinction between democracy as a form of government and democracy as an ideal community. I compare Dewey's social and political writings prior to his visit to China with his later works, arguing that Dewey's contact with the communal culture of China reinforced his belief about the essential value of community for democracy. His visit gave him the opportunity to cast aside the institutional baggage of Western democracy and to emphasize the idea of community life as a more secure foundation for democracy. This chapter ends with the implications of my study for the recent scholarship on Deweyan pragmatism and classical Confucianism, demonstrating that Dewey's own observations and appraisals of Chinese society can lend credence to the notion of "Confucian democracy" for China.

Chapter six offers suggestions for future research on Dewey and China. I believe that my work opens up new dimensions in Dewey scholarship. One may reinvestigate Dewey's relationships with his Chinese disciples or other Chinese intellectuals. One may also study the potential link between the entire body of Dewey's later philosophy and his visit to China, engage Dewey and Confucius in a dialogue on democracy, or explore the relevance of Dewey's reflections on internationalism to contemporary ethics of globalization.

CHAPTER 2

DEWEY AS A TEACHER

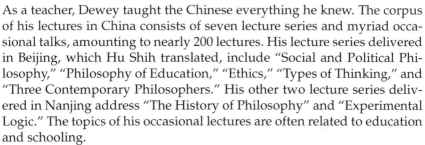

As a teacher, Dewey taught the Chinese everything he knew. The corpus of his lectures in China consists of seven lecture series and myriad occasional talks, amounting to nearly 200 lectures. His lecture series delivered in Beijing, which Hu Shih translated, include "Social and Political Philosophy," "Philosophy of Education," "Ethics," "Types of Thinking," and "Three Contemporary Philosophers." His other two lecture series delivered in Nanjing address "The History of Philosophy" and "Experimental Logic." The topics of his occasional lectures are often related to education and schooling.

All of these lectures were interpreted and recorded in Chinese as Dewey delivered them and were later printed in newspapers and reprinted in periodicals. In addition to these lectures, Dewey's own books, including *School and Society* (1899), *Schools of Tomorrow* (1915), *Democracy and Education* (1916), and *Reconstruction in Philosophy* (1920), were translated into Chinese and made available to the public during the early 1920s. As the first foreign scholar to be invited formally to lecture in China, Dewey became an instant celebrity. Wherever he went, he drew hundreds, and sometimes thousands, of people to his lectures. As one U.S. journalist in Shanghai reported, "It may be guessed that by means of the spoken and the written, or printed, word Professor Dewey has said his say to several hundred thousand Chinese."[1] To the Chinese, Dewey's lectures held the secrets to modern progress. If they could only know those secrets, they could build a modern China as powerful and prosperous as the United States.

Dewey as a Modern Confucius

In October 19, 1919, a banquet was held in Beijing to celebrate Dewey's sixtieth birthday—which happened to fall on the same day as the lunar birthday of Confucius. At the banquet, the Chancellor of Beijing University, Cai Yuanpei, seized on this special opportunity to portray Dewey as a modern-day Confucius. In his brief speech, Cai emphasized underlying similarities between Dewey and Confucius despite their differences: one embodies the spirit of modern West, and the other represents the wisdom of ancient China; one values democracy, equality, and creativity, and the other privileges monarchy, hierarchy, and tradition. According to Cai, Dewey and Confucius were both educators of the common people, shared the same faith in education as a vehicle for social change, and insisted on the unity of thought and action. Cai believed that these commonalities pointed to the possibility of "a merger between Eastern and Western cultures."[2] Interestingly, Dewey did not enjoy the honorific title exclusively—Bertrand Russell was also esteemed by his Chinese hosts as the "Second Confucius."[3] However, in terms of temperament and thought, Dewey was far more congenial to Confucius than Russell, who actually favored Daoism over Confucianism and found Confucius boring.[4]

Regardless of whether the comparison of Dewey to Confucius was appropriate, it took on a unique meaning in May Fourth China. Dewey was expected to take the discredited place of Confucius and assert himself as the new intellectual icon. Dewey's presence as the embodiment of Western modernity served as a potent source of inspiration for May Fourth intellectuals who were eager to jettison their old tradition and follow the Western path. The spirit of iconoclasm was best exemplified in Chen Duxiu, who proclaimed, to follow "Mr. Democracy," one should oppose Confucianism; to follow "Mr. Science," one should oppose traditional arts and religion.[5] In the eyes of many Chinese, Dewey came to embody "Mr. Science" and "Mr. Democracy."

The following discusses the content of Dewey's lectures in relation to his images in China. Dewey's experimental theory of inquiry made him well qualified as "Mr. Science." His promotion of democratic ideals earned him the legitimate title of "Mr. Democracy." His concerns for the education of the masses contributed to his reputation as the common people's educator. The three topics on science, democracy, and education are chosen for many reasons. First, they constitute the major themes of Dewey's lectures; second, they reflected the interests and concerns of his Chinese hosts; and third, they evoked considerable responses and criticisms from his audience. Dewey occasionally may have presented different schools of thought in an overly simplistic manner to make his lectures readily accessible to his Chinese audience.[6] I summarize Dewey's discussion of these themes, my purpose being interpretive rather than critical.

Dewey as "Mr. Science"

Dewey's image as "Mr. Science" owes to the fact that he advocates an experimental, scientific method of inquiry in solving social problems and emphasizes the positive impact of modern science on mental outlook. In his lectures on "Types of Thinking," Dewey discussed Aristotle's classic method of systematization and classification, Descartes's method of rationalistic deduction, and Locke's method of empirical sense perception, along with a new trend in modern thinking that he characterized as experimental. Dewey asserted that thinking in the modern epoch must reflect the progress in experimental science if we are to gain control over our environment and to replace superstition with intelligence as the governing force in human life. If the scientific method is not rendered serviceable to ordinary human experience, the predicaments in human society would remain unresolved. Unless the experimental method of inquiry is readily applied to the social, moral, and political spheres of life, the development of human civilizations would be arrested.

Dewey highlighted the contribution of Darwinism to modern thinking, urging his audience to discard the old view of a static nature, society, and man and to accept the newer concept of a dynamic universe dramatically illustrated in Darwin's account of the evolution of species. According to Dewey, Darwin's theory emancipates human thinking and imagination from worshipping the fixed and the permanent—hitherto ideal and perfect. Dewey called for a new pragmatic outlook—one that emphasizes the changing, the multiple, the heterogeneous, and the particular. He presented an account of truth and knowledge grounded in the context of a complete act of reflective inquiry. In his formulation, ideas should not be judged as antecedently true because they mirror an external reality, but should be regarded as hypotheses to be tested and verified in action. The efficacious method and procedures of modern experimental science present themselves as a paradigm of the reliable acquisition and critical evaluation of knowledge. The experimental method leads to a new conception of knowledge responsive to the dynamic contingencies and complexities of modern reality. Experimental thinking, Dewey said, is "not to produce useless or 'ornamental' knowledge," but to "make knowledge and practice more practical," thus "rendering human behavior more intelligent, more effectively controlled by reliable knowledge."[7]

Dewey knew that in their attempt to emulate Western technology, the Chinese tended to espouse a one-sided, mechanistic view of science, paying attention merely to the products, not the process, of science. Therefore, in his lectures, Dewey stressed science as a method of thinking, knowing, and acting that has a positive impact on morals and values. As he explained, people in primitive societies were pessimistic about and acquiescent to their surrounding environment because they did not see themselves as having any control over the environment. Superstition and fatalism were the key features of their lives. Progress in science enabled people to unlock the secrets of nature and to improve the material conditions of their lives. In this respect, modern science "introduced new hope into life" and "provided the basis for new courage in living."[8] Science also increased the human ability to judge truth from falsity, thus endowing honesty with a new meaning. Therefore, "the authority of tradition" should be replaced by "the authority of science."[9] The former is dictated by habit, consolidated by myths, and enjoyed only by a privileged few, whereas the latter is based on the observation of facts and openness to public scrutiny.

However, Dewey did not deny that advancement in modern technology and science had created some dire consequences—that is, the production of destructive weapons—which made the Chinese suspicious of its value. During his visit, Dewey was often asked about ways China could avoid the pitfalls of Western materialistic culture. He admitted that love of money, cruelty in military battles, and contention between capital and labor accompanied material progress in the West. Nonetheless, he believed that the remedy did not lie in the rejection of science but in a better understanding of what science means—especially of its moral and intellectual implications. Dewey hoped that the Chinese would come to appreciate science as a method of intelligence for coping with problems and difficulties in ordinary life, rather than as a collection of objective truths. Knowing that such a view of science was not even widely shared in the West, he somehow hoped that the Chinese would consider his suggestions, particularly when they planned for education reform. Dewey's view of science is interwoven with his belief in democracy and education. Only when children in schools learn to cultivate a sound habit of scientific thinking can schools be truly educational and society be truly democratized.

Dewey as "Mr. Democracy"

One of the most well-known and influential lectures Dewey gave in China was his first public lecture in Beijing in June 1919, "Democratic Developments in America," which was printed in six newspapers and periodicals in the same month. In this lecture, Dewey gave a historical account of the birth of U.S. democracy, preceded by an explication on the meaning of democracy. Dewey categorized democratic ideals into four dimensions: political, civil, economic, and social. Political democracy refers to the function of a republican government to secure public opinion.

Democracy in the civic sense ensures freedom of speech, movement, and association. Economic democracy is concerned with inequalities in standards of living. Social democracy aims to break down social hierarchies to allow all to develop to their fullest potential.[10] Dewey's broad delineation of democracy served two purposes. First, it pointed to the fact that democracy should affect all spheres of society; second, it encouraged the Chinese to develop plans for democratization according to their own circumstances and needs.

As Dewey reminded, democratic developments were not identical everywhere. American democracy was developed out of its unique history, geography, and psychology, as were other democracies. Dewey said that the British valued democracy because it secured individual freedom from constraints; the French supported democracy because it ensured equality for all. Even though the British and the French both practiced democracy, they each developed their own emphases according to the special circumstances, customs, and challenges that their societies faced. Dewey insisted that political ideals should reflect the actual facts of a given society and manifest its internal strengths and aspirations. Blindly following others' political ideals would not work, he warned. As far as the American example was concerned, Dewey said that Americans in the early colonial period did not trust big government; they valued self-reliance and thrived on self-government. The best government was thought to be one that governs the least. However, Dewey pointed out a growing awareness that the government had an important role to play in redressing the injustice of a laissez-faire economy and in answering the calls of workers for a more equitable distribution of wealth and a more equitable share in the management of public affairs. In spite of this concern, local control and grassroots activism still characterized the democratic spirit in the United States.

Dewey claimed that the government exists as an instrument to serve the needs of the people, not as an ultimate end or unquestionable good. Democracy is the only way to ensure that people's needs and interests are adequately expressed and addressed in the political process. Political elites, however wise and benevolent, are most likely to remain out of touch with the people and to abuse their power to serve their own interests. Dewey said that individual achievement or fulfillment should not be regarded as the highest goal of democracy; a new emphasis should be placed on the well-being of society as a whole that in turn contributes to the development of the individual. The American democratic ideal, Dewey noted, is to reinforce democracy through education and education through democracy. The spread of public education and the availability of equal educational opportunities mark a huge step toward the realization of this goal. Dewey assured his audience that democracy is the best means to prevent violent political disruptions and social revolutions.

In his lectures on "Social and Political Philosophy," Dewey explained the functions of social theory, the role of science in social philosophy, the origin of social conflict, the function of the state, the methods of social reform, and the criteria for evaluating social institutions and political regimes.[11] He began by rejecting all metaphysical explanations concerning the origins of theories, insisting that theories arise in times of actual social crisis or disintegration. They function "to provide solidarity for ways of thinking and doing" and to "generate faith" particularly in times of crisis.[12] Dewey observed that the prevalence of political slogans in the Great War was an example of how grand theories could actually make people sacrifice their property and even their lives. Because theories can cause significant consequences, people should be careful about what they choose to believe. Dewey claimed that the present age needed a reconstructed social and political philosophy.

According to Dewey, traditional social and political theories tend to fall into extremes: either too radical or too conservative. In terms of social change, the former rejects all old habits, customs, and institutions and aims to start everything anew, whereas the latter clings to traditions and resists sweeping changes. Dewey proposed a third alternative—a pragmatic, experimental, and particularistic approach—to the solving of concrete, specific problems as they arise in particular situations and at particular times. Traditional philosophies tend to be general, abstract, and absolute; modern philosophy, Dewey insisted, must incorporate the scientific method and eschew doctrinaire positions that overlook or deny the complexity of human affairs. According to this new philosophy, progress should be seen as "cumulative, a step forward here, a bit of improvement there," as "piecemeal, not all at once," and as "retail business, not wholesale."[13] The goal is to replace sudden and violent revolution with steady and cumulative changes based on the increase in social knowledge and intelligence. The alternative to revolution as a means to social progress is "a system of habits, customs, conventions, traditions, and institutions flexible enough to permit adjustment to changing environments and conditions."[14]

Dewey repudiated earlier theories that pit the individual against society or people against the government. Instead, he claimed that social conflicts arise from an imbalance of interests between groups—between those whose interests are well acknowledged and served by society at large and others whose interests are largely neglected. To distinguish his ideas from Marx's narrow categories of the bourgeois versus the proletariat, Dewey clarified what he meant by "groups," namely, those constituted along economic as well as occupational, ideational, or ethnic lines. Dewey said that social conflicts often occur when the interests of some groups are gained at the disadvantage, or the suppression, of the interest of other groups. To resolve conflicts, people must devise means for bringing the interests of all groups into balance, providing all with the opportunity to develop so that each can contribute to the common good. Dewey underscored the fundamental interdependence of all social groups by stating that "any real advantage of one group is shared by all groups; and when one group suffers disadvantage, all are hurt."[15]

Dewey argued that a pragmatic and experimental approach to politics, as opposed to either the radical or the conservative, provides a framework within which leaders of reform movements can adopt an attitude of inquiry when solving social problems. He said that "when leaders of reform movements can thoughtfully diagnose the ills and deficiencies of their society, reform becomes a matter of advocating methods for correcting ills and satisfying deficiencies, and not of revolution which undertakes to scrap the whole structure of existing institutional arrangements."[16] The criterion for judging social habits, customs, and institutions lies in whether they contribute to associated living, characterized by open communication and exchange of ideas, and by mutual respect, friendship, and love. Because a democratic society is one that promotes social communication and interaction among individuals, it depends for its stability and development not on military force, but on consensus. A society organized along master-slave relationships contains within itself the seeds of its own destruction because it depends on force for its existence—which is sure to result in resistance. Constitutional democracy incorporates within its very structure guarantees that its members will have opportunity to pursue their own interests. Because members of such a society recognize that they have a stake in it, social order will persist relatively unimpaired when a change in government takes place. In this respect, democracy is the most stable form of government, Dewey claimed. It is not only capable of securing the unity of a social organism, but is also the best means to this end.

On economics, Dewey criticized individualistic, laissez-faire economies, which he believed led to the debacle of war. He was sympathetic to socialism in general and saw the end of the nineteenth century as demarcating the legitimacy of government control in regulating industry. Dewey said that even among the many socialist theories, they shared "the conviction that economic activities should be conducted to the end of common welfare, not primarily for individual profit."[17] However, Dewey denounced Marxism for discarding all moral and ethical considerations and questioned its applicability to the Chinese. Instead, he suggested guild socialism as a better way to prevent the conflict between labor and capital and to develop industry along democratic lines. In addition, Dewey thought that socialism need not focus only on economic questions. He envisioned a different kind of socialism based on equal opportunities to share intangible things as knowledge, ideas, and experiences. As Dewey explained, "Where material things are concerned, the more people who share them, the less each will have, but the opposite is true of knowledge. The store of knowledge is increased by the number of people who come to share in it. Knowledge can be shared and increased at the same time—in fact, it is increased by being shared."[18]

Dewey was aware of the increasing trend toward individualism in China and was wary of its concomitant problems. He advised the Chinese not to follow the same path Western nations had taken—namely, going through a stage of self-seeking individualism to the next stage in which state power had to be used to ensure social equality. Dewey hoped that China could "amalgamate these two steps and achieve equality at one stroke." China could achieve social equality by using its own social foundations and philosophical traditions: "Political individualism has not made headway in China, so that the tradition of the state's obligation to protect its people [as propounded by Mencius], which may be likened to the parents' obligation to protect their children, or the emperor to protect his subjects, can readily be modified into the concept of protection of its citizens by a democratic government."[19] Dewey believed that Chinese culture was endowed with democratic elements that would enable her to carry out the transition to industrialism more creatively and effectively than the West had done.

Dewey as the Common People's Educator

Dewey's first lecture in China was on democratic education. He stated that education in the modern era is not the privilege of a select few but a right to which every citizen is entitled. It should contribute to the betterment of common people's lives. Indeed, Dewey was rightly honored as the common people's educator, championing a new vision of education for a modern society.

In his lectures on "Philosophy of Education," Dewey pointed out the importance of a philosophy of education in a progressive society—as opposed to a conservative one—because it serves to guard against "blind subservience to custom" and "slavish imitation."[20] Inherent tendencies to fear the new and unfamiliar and to shy away from difficulty and criticism characterize conservative societies. Progressive societies, on the contrary, encourage people to seek the novel, take risks, and assume responsibility. Modern education should abandon the remnants of elitism, maintain a balanced curriculum between literary training and practical living, and cultivate ingenuity and creativity. With the development of new educational aims, educators should abandon traditional methods of teaching, that is, simply passing knowledge to children without any regard for how it relates to the practical life outside of school.

Influenced by antiquated theories of knowledge, traditional education assumes the child to be passive and views the mind as a receptacle to be filled. Traditional schools isolate academic subjects and force ready-made history, geography, and other subjects into the child's mind. They employ methods of learning largely confined to memorization, recitation, and examination. Traditional education thus breeds an aristocracy of learning and develops an exaggerated regard for antiquity. New education, on the other hand, assumes the child to be active and views learning as resulting from innate interests and dispositions. Knowledge is seen as an instrument for guiding conduct, and its acquisition as a means to solving problems in practical life. The goal of schools is to help students identify and resolve problems they encounter in actual life.

Dewey criticized the separation of intellectual training with moral cultivation. The separation would inevitably remain as long as teachers continue to pass on knowledge to students and isolate learning from doing. Dewey also opposed direct moral instruction, insisting that that even though the cultivation of moral character is the goal of education, treating moral education as a separate phase of the curriculum is a pedagogical error. Neither knowledge nor morality can be imparted by one person to another. Instead, the spirit of service should permeate the entire curriculum and atmosphere of the school. The school should "cultivate individuality in such ways as will enhance the individual's social sympathy."[21] It should help develop persons with character, judgment, and a sense of social responsibility.

Although Dewey affirmed the role of vocational education in China's industrial development, he insisted that it should not be reduced to a mechanical training for a special trade. It is wrong to treat certain people as being born for certain jobs and to "accept present conditions in business or industry as our standard."[22] Dewey suggested that vocational education should provide training in the scientific method and enable people to appreciate the interrelationships and interdependence of all social occupations. Because social conditions change and technological progress is rapid, preparing children in school to perform specific jobs does not make sense. As for the proper relationship between education and industry, Dewey said that industry should provide the school with problems and materials for investigation, and the school should in turn cultivate skills and talents that would improve industrial development. A good vocational education must have a technical as well as an intellectual dimension.

Dewey's call for a new mental outlook in keeping with the advancement in experimental science, his proposal for a pragmatic theory of truth and knowledge that unites thought and action, his insistence on the role of intelligence in human affairs, his emphasis on education as a vehicle for social change, his practical pedagogical suggestions, and his vision of democracy as a way of life—all of these were meant to be general guidelines for social reconstruction in China.

Dewey as a Democratic Teacher

In spite of the various titles and images associated with him, Dewey saw himself simply as a teacher. But what kind of a teacher was he? How well did he meet the needs of his Chinese hosts and audience? Did he live up to the ideal of a democratic teacher? Did he leave any enduring messages behind?

When viewing Dewey's lectures in China, one scholar made the following comment: "The references to the Chinese people are few and, for the most part, not revealing of a deep understanding of the cultural, economic or political life of China. With a few changes, a different example here or there, the lectures might have been delivered at any university in the U.S."[23] Obviously, the reviewer simply relied on Clopton and Ou's book to make this judgment. However, the lectures they translated comprise only one-sixth of the entire corpus of Dewey's lectures and were delivered only in the first year of his stay. Although Dewey's major lecture series are theory-based, his occasional lectures are context-based and contain frequent references to contemporary Chinese situations. For example, when Dewey was visiting the capital city of Hunan, he learned of a social event during which students allegedly tore down religious statues to protest superstition and idol worship. Their behavior aroused strong reactions from the local residents and the educational authorities concerned. Perhaps trying to mediate the dispute, Dewey addressed this issue in his lecture. While acknowledging the students' enthusiasm for change, he urged them to employ steady and constructive means to reconstruct society.[24] Contrary to the allegation that Dewey was inattentive to local situations, Dewey was highly aware of the events happening around him.

Dewey was always concerned with what China needed and what he could offer. For instance, when preparing for his lecture series, Dewey took Hu Shih's suggestion to start with social and political philosophy—a topic of great interest to the Chinese. Hu told Dewey that doing so would be a great opportunity for him to "formulate a coherent statement of a social and political philosophy based in pragmatism." Hu also reminded the Chinese audience of "their rare good fortune in sharing Dr. Dewey's initial formal statement of his social and political philosophy." Hu asked Dewey to consider publishing these lectures in English and volunteered to translate Dewey's manuscript into Chinese so that "both English and Chinese versions can be published at the same time."[25] Although a formal and systematic approach to politics, irrespective of the particularity of context, may seem inconsistent with pragmatism, Dewey agreed to start his lecture series on social and political philosophy—with his own plan, as he said to a friend, to provide an "outline of the whole field."[26]

Dewey's choice to introduce William James, Henri Bergson, and Bertrand Russell for his lecture series on "Three Contemporary Philosophers" also reflects his willingness to accommodate the interests of his hosts and audience. Not familiar with the background of Dewey's visit in China, one scholar actually finds Dewey's selection of the three "contemporary" philosophers rather amusing:

> James had been dead for nine years, and Dewey justified his inclusion by the comment that his works were having their greatest impact at the moment. Bergson was a logical choice; he was alive and famous. . . . One might add that Dewey was not partial to metaphysicians, either. But I doubt that his choice were a matter of personal taste, because that might have led him to omit Russell, too, despite Russell's meteoric career and extraordinary brilliance. Perhaps Dewey was trying to show his Oriental audience what he believed and hoped about man and society and was talking about those fellow philosophers who shared the same beliefs and hopes.[27]

Even though Dewey's selection may seem strange to scholars today, it made perfect sense to the Chinese—especially when we consider the special circumstances of the time and the particular ideological interests of different groups—the liberal, the traditionalist, and the socialist.

The liberal camp Hu Shih led favored William James because they could use his theory of truth to legitimize their attack on traditional Chinese culture. The traditionalists, on the other hand, were drawn to the philosophy of Henri Bergson because they took his creative theory of evolution as affirming the spiritual dimension of human life. His theory was appealing to those who, after the Great War, became disillusioned with the scientific and materialistic culture of the West and wanted to call for a return to their own spiritual traditions.[28] Dewey's introduction of Bergson consolidated his reputation among traditionalist supporters. In the well-known controversy over Eastern and Western civilizations, Bergson's mystic style and his emphasis on intuition over intellect served as a powerful source of inspiration and authority for the traditionalists. In fact, Bergson was invited to lecture in China after Dewey and Russell, but the visit did not materialize. Although James and Bergson were favored respectively by the liberals and the traditionalists, Bertrand Russell was a hero to the radicals. His social and political thought—as represented in major works such as *Principles of Social Reconstruction* (1916), *Political Ideals* (1917), *Roads to Freedom: Socialism, Anarchism, and Syndicalism* (1918),

The Theory and Practice of Bolshevism (1920)—had an immense appeal to the Chinese who supported socialism and opposed capitalism and imperialism. Because Russell was invited to lecture in China in the fall of 1920, Dewey's introduction of him may have been intended to pave the way for his reception. In hindsight, we can see that Dewey's selection of these three philosophers—one American, one French, and one British—to meet the respective ideological interests of the liberal, the traditionalist, and the socialist in May Fourth China, was quite appropriate.

Whenever he could, Dewey would tailor his occasional talks to meet the interests and the needs of his audiences. For instance, when Dewey was invited to speak at Beijing University on the twenty-second anniversary of its founding, he spoke about the responsibility of a university in generating well-informed and enlightened public opinion in a democracy. When he attended the inauguration of a student government at Beijing Teachers' College, he lectured on student self-government and assured the students that open discussion of events leads to better decisions than the unchallenged reasoning of a few wise men. When invited to speak at a College of Law and Administration, Dewey chose to talk about the foundation of democratic politics. He reminded the students that political rights need to be earned and that political democracy is a continuous process, not fully realized even in the West. When talking to teachers at normal schools, Dewey addressed pedagogical issues, such as the importance of spontaneity in learning, and he encouraged teachers to assume leadership in reforming society. When visiting a high school, Dewey lectured on civic education and urged the students to cooperate with one another to pursue common goals. Most interesting, Dewey even managed to give a talk on Chinese fine arts. In this lecture addressed to students interested in fine arts, Dewey not only acknowledged the intrinsic value of the arts, but he also encouraged the students to explore the relevance of classic arts to contemporary life to enhance the quality of living for all.[29]

Because Dewey lectured frequently during his two-year stay, repetition was inevitable. He expressed concern about this as he pondered whether to stay in China for a second year. "I have done all the general lecturing I can, said all that can be said of a general sort I mean, and as they have been published all over China—remember the four hundred million, I [can't] say the same thing over again next year very well."[30] Dewey finally agreed to stay on the condition that his general lecturing load would be reduced and his major responsibility would be to teach regular courses at the host universities. However, he frequently received lecture invitations even when he was about to depart the country. In his last public lecture in Beijing, Dewey began by saying that because he had given so many lectures, he actually had nothing much to add. However, he felt reluctant to decline the invitation and thus agreed to give a farewell speech.[31] Throughout the course of his visit, Dewey hardly complained about the arrangements made for him except that when asked to give a talk on religion, he declined. He told his close friend about this event:

> I was invited to speak on religion and declined and the secy [*sic*] of the student society which invited me came around to see me and naively said they wanted to get the question settled while Russell and I were in the country. Of course it [isn't] all as bad as this, but in a way [it's] typical. Russell gave out an interview in which he remarked that in the Western world no one had any faith any longer in the "wise men" but China was still in the stage where it believed that a wise man could come along and settle its difficulties and questions.[32]

Interestingly, Dewey added, Russell "got on to the weak points of the Chinese in much shorter time than I did."[33]

Even though Dewey had great sympathy for the struggles of the Chinese and admired many unique qualities of Chinese culture, he was not uncritical of their weaknesses—their passivity and reliance on authority. Therefore, in his lectures, he often stressed the importance of spontaneity, creativity, and initiative, reminding his audience that they needed to reconcile partisan disputes and undertake practical tasks that demands large-scale organization and cooperation. Dewey also said that their reliance on authority prevented them from taking charge and engaging in social experimentation. Knowing that the Chinese had not learned to organize themselves to operate on a national level, Dewey suggested that schools should cultivate a sense of public spirit extending beyond the students' immediate environments. As Dewey approached the end of his sojourn in China, he felt compelled to urge the Chinese to overcome their passivity and sense of helplessness.

In May 1921, Dewey gave a speech titled, "Self-Activity and Self-Government," stating, "Classical education encourages passivity; it might be all right for puppets, but not appropriate for children capable of spontaneity and initiative; it served very well for the time when it evolved, but it cannot meet today's needs." He maintained, "the only way that the problems which now beset China will ever be solved is by the spontaneous efforts of the Chinese people themselves."[34] In July 1921, immediately before Dewey's departure, he gave a talk on "The Importance of Dynamic Morality." He said, "the static and passive morality which is characteristic of the Chinese people may produce strong and enduring character, but it stresses obedience and filial piety; dynamic morality, on the other hand, stresses creativity, venturesomeness and willingness to assume responsibility." Dewey argued that static and passive morality was appropriate for an authoritarian state; but "in a democratic state where maintenance of social equilibrium and progress of social reconstruction are functions of individual responsibility, dynamic morality must be cultivated."[35] China's survival, Dewey insisted, hinged on the cultivation of dynamic morality through schooling.

An additional point about Dewey's lecture schedules in China is worth noting. Dewey's major lectures series were delivered on Friday evenings, Saturday afternoons, and Sunday mornings, perhaps to accommodate the schedule of his translator. Dewey's schedule of traveling was also extensive. He traveled to eleven provinces in China, some of which he even visited twice. In mid-April 1921, three months before he was to leave the country, he was invited to lecture in Fujian, a province in southern China. However, during his trip, he learned that some students in Beijing were using his name to protest against taking any examinations. He decided to return to Beijing hastily to clear up the misunderstanding. These details might seem minor, but when we consider the traveling conditions of the time, along with the fact that such an intensive schedule was demanding of a sixty-year-old man, the tribute to Dewey as a modern Confucius was, in fact, well deserved. We may further appreciate Dewey's benevolence toward the Chinese if we compare him with China's other guest at the time, Bertrand Russell.

Unlike Dewey who was so accommodating to the expectations of his Chinese hosts and so attentive to the needs of his audience, Bertrand Russell showed impatience with the arrangements made for him on his arrival. He refused to meet the expectations of all to hear him lecture on his book *Principles of Social Reconstruction*—something to which the entire intellectual circle had been looking forward when they learned that he had agreed to visit China. Much to their disappointment, Russell decided to begin his lectures with technical philosophy, starting with "The Problems of Philosophy," "The Analysis of Mind," "The Analysis of Matter," and then "Mathematical Logic." Yet Russell complained to his friend in a letter that the Chinese were not interested in pure philosophy, and all they wanted were concrete suggestions on how to reform their society.[36] Even when Russell finally agreed to lecture on social theories, he decided to change the topic from "Principles of Social Reconstruction"—long anticipated by the Chinese—to "The Science of Social Structure." He stressed that he would be presenting a "scientific account" of the relationship between social change and social structure. As one Chinese scholar pointed out, Russell chose to lecture on "The Science of Social Structure" probably to avoid getting into too much controversy.[37]

In contrast to Dewey who traveled extensively, Russell stayed primarily in Beijing. Unlike Dewey who extended his stay in China from a few months to two years, Russell shortened his visit from one full year to nine months. In fact, four months into his stay, Russell began to feel bored because everything seemed to have become a routine to him. He also felt that discussing philosophy with Chinese students was pointless because their understanding was very limited. He thought that the students "don't work hard and have not much brains," although they were "friendly and enthusiastic."[38] He thought that "most of the students were stupid and timid" and that they needed "board-school teachers, not eminent professors."[39] However, the students seemed to think of Russell "as an amiable old fogy."[40] They were treating him and Dora Black like an emperor and an empress and were honoring their love out of wedlock by promoting what was called "Russell Marriage."[41] Nonetheless, Russell still thought that Beijing was as isolating as a dead pond, and that if one stayed too long in it, one's mind would be retarded.[42] Later, in March 1921, he caught pneumonia, became seriously ill for three months, and had to cancel all lecture plans. After he fully recovered in July, Russell decided that the time had come to depart the country. After giving a farewell speech on "China's Road to Freedom," Russell and his mistress left Beijing on July 11, 1921, reportedly on the same day as Dewey and his wife.

Russell's message to the Chinese in his farewell address conflicts with his initial remarks about Bolshevism. In his first lecture on "The Bolsheviks and World Politics," Russell told the Chinese that he "did not approve of the Bolsheviks" because their authoritarian regime resorted to violence as a means to consensus.[43] He said that even though communism was a good theory, it should not be implemented hastily or forcefully. The views Russell expressed in this lecture were consistent with his book *The Theory and Practice of Bolshevism*, which he wrote after visiting Soviet Russia and before traveling to China. Russell's criticism of Bolshevism aroused strong reactions from those Chinese who were enthusiastic about the Bolshevik regime and were gradually converting to communism. As Dewey also revealed in his letter, "[Russell's] criticisms of Bolshevism rather weakened the attachment of students."[44] Chen Duxiu was an example. Chen, who proclaimed to be following "Mr. Science" and "Mr. Democracy" in early 1919, had become the secretary of the Chinese Communist Party secretly founded in May 1920. On hearing Russell's negative comments about Bolshevism, Chen wrote a letter to Russell, asking him to clarify his views about Bolshevism "to avoid the disappointment of the Chinese people in you."[45] Whether Russell received Chen's letter is not known.

However, in his second speech, "Bolshevik Thought," given one month later, Russell was no longer critical of Bolshevism. He portrayed it in a positive light by saying that Bolshevism was concerned with enforcing justice in gender, international, economic, and social relations. Russell also reiterated his faith in communism, claiming that even though the

Russians had encountered some problems, "the world should support them," and "every civilized nation in the world should try to put this wonderful theory into practice."[46] In light of the controversies caused by his previous remarks, Russell seemed careful not to agitate the radicals who supported Bolshevism—only to find himself attacked in turn by those who favored anarchism, syndicalism, or guild socialism. In his farewell address, "China's Road to Freedom," Russell addressed the topic of Bolshevism again—after many months of lectures largely on pure philosophy. In this speech, he claimed that although Bolshevism was not applicable to Europe, the case in China was different. He suggested that the Chinese adopt state socialism and follow the example of the Russian Bolsheviks in developing industry and popularizing education.[47]

Russell's three lectures on Bolshevism often contradicted themselves. This may have resulted from inadequate translation as well as the inconsistencies in Russell's own thoughts. We can note the problem of translation from a letter Dewey wrote in which he mentioned overhearing Russell's speech on "The Bolsheviks and World Politics":

> [Russell] lectured this p m right after I did, on Bolshevism. I was rushed right out of the hall, to "go and get rested." I suppose from politeness but it almost looked as if they [didn't] want me to hear him. I judge they are about the same as his articles. The only thing I heard him say was that one reason he was opposed to Bolshevism was that the rest of the world [wouldn't] accept it voluntarily, they were bound to impose it, and that would mean continued fighting and he considered the situation so precarious that civilization might go under in a prolonged war. The other thing was that they were doing a lot for the children.[48]

Two of Russell's comments on Bolshevism, which Dewey claimed to overhear, did not appear in the Chinese text. The text contained only the statement that Russell did not approve of Bolshevism, but the reasons for his disapproval, as Dewey described, were not mentioned.

The inconsistencies in Russell's lectures, regardless of whether they were caused by his own shifting thoughts or by problematic translation, generated heated debates within the socialist camp. Confused as well as frustrated, fervent socialists were disputing among themselves about which school of socialism Russell truly endorsed: anarcho-syndicalism, guild socialism, state socialism, or Bolshevism. Contenders on different sides of the debate used evidence from different speeches, or even different parts of the same speech, to claim that Russell agreed with them. In fact, for the most part, Russell was himself divided in his own attitudes toward Bolshevism. As he described in a letter, "My disapproval of Bolshevism, in so far as I do disapprove, is on the ground that I do not think it can achieve the ends at which it aims. I regard the Bolsheviks as 'knights of the impossible,' and the whole development of Russia during the last 3 years confirms me in this view. It is as a practical man, not as an idealist, that I object to them."[49] When Russell spoke negatively about Bolshevism, he was being "practical"; when he spoke positively, he was being "idealistic."

Unlike Russell, Dewey did not sever theory from practice. He also would not support any theory not firmly grounded in practice. Dewey was particularly right about Russell "being constitutionally in opposition"—he "could write a wonderful critique on either heaven or hell after a short stay in either."[50] Most significantly, excluding the possibility of problematic translation, what Russell suggested to the Chinese in the his farewell speech on "China's Road to Freedom" contradicted what he said to the English reading public in his *The Problem of China* (1922), in which he claimed that "Bolshevism, as it has developed in Russia, is quite peculiarly inapplicable to China."[51] Unlike Russell who seemed self-contradictory and opportunistic, however eloquent and charismatic, Dewey remained consistent and truthful in his presentation of the Chinese to the West and of the West to the Chinese.

As Remer pointed out insightfully in 1920, what Dewey was trying to do in China was "to get the thoughtless and the conservative to look upon the experimental method with more hope and less fear and get the enthusiastic critic to develop within himself some discipline and some test to distinguish between what is desirable and what is not." Remer further wrote, "[Dewey's] way is democratic because it depends upon the development of standards within the citizen and not upon the imposition of standards from without upon the subject. His way is the liberal and the tolerant way. The autocrat and the doctrinaire cannot use it. Dewey can do no more than to make it clear and to say it again and again as he goes about in this country."[52] Dewey's democratic stance toward the Chinese will be more evident when we later discuss his role as a learner in chapter four.

Those who were familiar with Dewey appreciated his contribution to Chinese education as well as his sincerity and kindness. At the farewell banquet held for Dewey, one female professor from a teachers' college thanked Dewey for helping to change traditional Chinese attitudes toward education. People used to respect teachers but not the teaching profession itself because they thought that anybody could be a teacher. Dewey's advocacy for teaching as a profession was a corrective to the traditional laissez-faire attitude toward teaching because he encouraged teachers to examine the underlying principles of their teaching so that they could avoid blind subservience to tradition or slavish imitation of foreign ideas. Moreover, she said:

Dewey was not only teaching us; he was teaching Europeans and Americans about us. There have been politicians and diplomats in the country before. However, their reports about us were usually distorted by their own particular interests and agenda. Many came to visit for a few days and returned with a book of one or two thousand pages. Dewey was different. He reported our situations truthfully to the reading public in America. He would occasionally point out our problems and weaknesses, but he had great love for us.[53]

Dewey returned the kindness of his Chinese hosts by acknowledging that he had a wonderful time and learned very much from his visit. He stressed his admiration for the young people in China—their enthusiasm for new learning and their concern with the well-being of society at large—but he kindly reminded the Chinese that the problems of China could be solved only by actually trying to solve them. It was pointless, Dewey noted, to wait until one figures out whether a good government should precede good education or vice versa. In Dewey's opinion, the young intelligentsia "were surfeited with theories," including his own.[54] As a teacher, Dewey had said all he had to say and the rest lay with the Chinese themselves to solve their own problems. Indeed, China could not have asked for a more benevolent and democratic teacher than John Dewey.

Whose Teaching? Or Hu's Teaching?

So far I have presented the content of Dewey's teaching as it appeared in the Chinese texts of his lectures without considering semantic or aesthetic distortions in the process of translation. Now I turn to whether these texts were unequivocal representations of what Dewey actually said and whether Hu Shih's "cultural-intellectualistic" approach to the reform of Chinese society was in keeping with Dewey's more pragmatic and practical stance.[55] The answers should urge us to reconsider whether Dewey was responsible for the failure of Hu's cultural reformism.

First of all, we should note that the existing English translation of Dewey's lectures is several times removed from the original. As the translators themselves noted, one needs to consider "the possibility of significant alterations in meaning in such a process."[56] Those who read the English translation may feel that the content is largely consistent with Dewey's thoughts. As one scholar remarks, "translations into English of what he [Dewey] reported to have said . . . sounded very like him and constitute a reliable primer of his philosophy."[57] However, the English translation contains only Dewey's lectures on "Social and Political Philosophy" and "Philosophy of Education." If we study Dewey's other lectures recorded in Chinese, we would be more likely to notice the problem of translation.

If one is both conversant with Dewey's style and familiar with Hu's writings, one can discern passages in which Hu's translations seem highly problematic—mostly in style and tone and occasionally in content. Hu's eloquent, pompous, and proselytizing style marked a dramatic difference from Dewey's usually unassuming and unimposing style. However, I do not mean to suggest that Hu Shih intended to distort Dewey's lectures, nor do I mean to imply that the records of Dewey's lectures in China were largely fabricated and unreliable. Nonetheless, we may reasonably believe that Hu may have occasionally altered the meanings of what Dewey said to highlight a particular point or to promote a certain agenda. Even though these occasional anomalies may seem minor, they eventually affected the way Chinese intellectuals responded to Dewey.

Let me start with a blatant example. In a highly anticipated and publicized lecture, "Democratic Developments in America," Dewey was reported to have said the following about U.S. society:

> Even though there has been an increasing gap between the rich and the poor, there is still equality between them. Why is this so? Because the poor still have the opportunity to get ahead through hard work; they can still get rich if they so aspire. Those who are rich do not look down on the poor. This is how social equality is maintained. There is not only no social hierarchy in American society; there is no gender hierarchy, either. The issue of gender hierarchy in China is very serious, whereas in the United States men and women are equal and there is no distinction between them at all.[58]

Dewey—who was active in promoting equal education for women and women's suffrage, and who once "marched in a suffrage parade unknowing carrying a banner thrust into its hands which read 'Men can vote! Why can't I?'"—probably would not have claimed that the United States was without gender hierarchy.[59] Additionally, Dewey—who had been involved with Jane Addams at Hull House in Chicago to campaign for social and labor reforms—probably would not have professed that his own country had no social inequality. When Dewey wrote home on June 5, 1919, he told his children, "in some ways there is more democracy than we have; leaving out the women, there is complete social equality."[60]

We do not know what Dewey said that led Hu to this interpretation. We cannot be sure whether this might have been a problem of inadequate recording rather than problematic translation. We obviously cannot rule out the possibility that Dewey might have described U.S. society in a positive light to impress his Chinese audience. However, the inconsistency I have shown is so glaring and so unlike Dewey that we need to consider multiple scenarios. I think we should give more weight to the fact that

Hu had always been "a steadfast defender and advocate of American values."[61] Therefore, his own idealized image of the United States may have affected his interpretation. Perhaps the details about U.S. society were not important to the Chinese as long as they were informed about the larger contours of its democratic development. Nevertheless, examples such as this often leave the impression that Dewey did not seem to be concerned with labor questions. It gave left-wing radicals sufficient grounds to denounce Dewey as "a defender of capitalists and the bourgeoisie."[62]

Dewey was far from unconcerned with the conditions of the poor. Two weeks after his arrival, he wrote home, noting the problem of "the extreme poverty of China," of which he was unaware before coming to the country.[63] In his lectures on "Social and Political Philosophy," Dewey emphasized the importance of building a solid economic infrastructure on which social life was to be built. Later in his stay, Dewey often reminded the Chinese to develop industry and improve the material conditions of their lives. However, as Chow points out, Dewey's discussion of China's economic problems did not "attract enough attention from his Chinese students and friends and other Chinese liberals" who were "preoccupied with educational reform, academic research and the re-evaluation of national classics."[64]

Another example shows how Hu Shih may have borrowed Dewey's authority to promote his own belief that China should assimilate itself fully with Western civilization, which he later spelled out as "total Westernization." According to the Chinese text, Dewey said, "China should no longer rely on the Great Wall to resist Western culture" and China "should open its door to absorb all the greatness of Western civilization" to redress the wrongs that had been done to China since Western intrusion.[65] Implied in this statement is Hu's fundamental belief in the superiority of Western civilization. As Chinese historian Lin Yu-sheng points out, Hu Shih thought that "the traditional Chinese mind was so diseased" that "it could not cure itself through its own resources. Its salvation was possible only after the advent of Western civilization on the Chinese scene."[66] Hu's rejection of traditional Chinese culture conflicts with Dewey's affirmation of its internal strengths. Dewey would not have agreed with Hu's totalistic antitraditionalism.[67] Dewey once wrote, "China has evolved, not borrowed, her civilization," and China's problem was not one of "successful borrowing" of foreign ideas—as in the case of Japan—but one "of transformation, of making over from within." Dewey hoped that the Chinese would not learn Western ideas "for the sake of getting models to pattern herself after, but to get ideas, intellectual capital, with which to renovate her own institutions" (MW 11: 207).

This example also helps us understand why Hu Shih's contemporary adversary, Mei Guangdi, accused him of "abducting" Dewey, of treating him like a "puppet," and of using Dewey to "increase his own fame" and to "destroy traditional Chinese culture entirely."[68] Interestingly, as a student of Irving Babbitt at Harvard University, Mei was devoted to promoting Babbitt's New Humanism as a counterforce against Hu Shih's pragmatism and his New Culture movement. Babbitt's call for a return to Greek and Roman classics reinforced Mei's belief in the preservation of traditional Chinese literature. However, Mei's writings were written in classical language and were not widely read.[69] Despite their differences, one can see that Hu and Mei both resorted to foreign authority to validate their own agendas. The dispute between Hu and Mei marked one instance among many in the larger battle between *cultural* radicals and conservatives. Another major controversy in this period was one between *political* radicals and conservatives. In this case, Hu's cultural radicalism contrasted with his political conservatism. We shall see how Hu used Dewey's lectures to advocate an intellectualistic reform approach as a more desirable alternative to radical social change.

As you may recall from my previous discussion of Dewey's lectures, he said that social and political philosophies tend to fall into extremes, either too radical or conservative. According to the Chinese text, Dewey stated, "*both* committed the same mistake of seeking a 'fundamental resolution.'" Appearing in quotation marks in the text, the term "fundamental resolution" has the connotation of a "sweeping and all-encompassing solution."[70] We do not know what Dewey actually said, but he may have held that both radicals and conservatives cling to a permanent and absolute solution to social problems without considering the need for continuous social experimentation. However, in Hu Shih's rendering, Dewey seemed to be criticizing only the radicals for attempting to resolve social problems by eradicating existing systems. Hu clearly seems to deliberately choose the term to denounce Marxist ideas promulgated by his opponent Li Dazhao.

At the time, Hu Shih was involved in a heated debate with Li—soon to become one of the founders of the Chinese Communist Party in 1920—over whether an all-encompassing solution to China's problems was possible and desirable. From July to September 1919, a series of polemical essays were exchanged between these two men that aroused tremendous attention in intellectual circles. It was later regarded as demarcating the first round of debates between pragmatism and Marxism. In his initial essay, "More Study of Problems and Less Talk of Isms," Hu deplored the radicals' uncritical interest in various kinds of socialist theories. Claiming that theories on paper were dangerous, Hu urged his fellow intellectuals to study concrete, specific problems, such as how to reform the family system, to liberate women, and to unite political factions. Hu vilified the radicals' insistence on a "fundamental resolution" by calling it "a sign of intellectual laziness," "a self-deceiving dream," "an ironclad proof of the bankruptcy of Chinese thought," and "a death-sentence to Chinese social reform."[71]

In his reply, Li Dazhao agreed that studying concrete, specific problems was important, but he chided Hu for being impractical. Hu's approach could not help promote a common consensus or generate a collective vision, which alone could move people to action. "Despite your vehement study of social problems," Li said, "these problems can never be solved because the majority of people in society do not feel related."[72] Li maintained that large-scale transformation of existing social and political structures was a prerequisite to the solving of all other problems that Hu indicated. The heart of their disagreement lies in whether China needed a radical revolution or gradual reform to resolve the political failure of the 1911 revolution.[73] Li believed in the Bolshevik regime in Russia, whereas Hu devoted himself to "literary revolution," that is, replacing the classical written language with the vernacular language as the new mode of public discourse and a new style of literature.

Even though Hu advocated less talk of "isms," he was also engaged in importing Western "isms" into the intellectual marketplace of China. In his own treatment of pragmatism, Hu drew heavily from William James, highlighting pragmatism as a theory of truth. His purpose was obvious—to attack traditional norms and beliefs. Even though Hu accurately understood and promoted Dewey's pragmatism as a method of social inquiry, Hu seemed to have missed the action component in Dewey's theory. Hu may have "learned from Dewey that the most sacred responsibility of a man's life is to endeavor to think well," as he once reflected.[74] However, he overlooked Dewey's call to unite thought and action and to integrate means and ends.

Owing to his personal temperament that better suited him to be a scholar rather than a social activist, Hu Shih did not study those concrete, practical problems he himself so eloquently identified. In the 1920s, Hu and some of his followers in the New Culture movement turned not to the study of practical social problems, but to "esoteric matters, such as archeological investigations, the study of ancient Chinese philosophy and history, and the textual criticisms of traditional literature."[75] In fact, one may doubt whether Hu Shih was fully committed to leading reform in China. Both Dewey and his wife revealed in their letters that Hu intended to return to the United States and obtain a teaching position at Columbia University. Alice was critical: "[Hu] is afraid if he stays here these political agitations will so prevent his doing concentrated work that he will get out of the habit. What do you think of that for intellectual logic in patriotism, in building up the foundations for a national intellectual life?"[76] Dewey, on the other hand, was more sympathetic: "I [don't] see how China can spare him, but it is rather pathetic to see how many of the old students here long for life in the US."[77]

However, the defeat of Hu's cultural reformism was often thought to be a result of Dewey's influence or a corollary of Dewey's pragmatism. Nancy Sizer speculates that Dewey's presence—"the presence of the 'master' himself" as she puts it—might have prevented his students from "the flexible, innovative treatment of the philosophy which would have made possible its adaptation to Chinese culture."[78] Maurice Meisner argues that "applied to China, Dewey's program was neither conservative nor radical but largely irrelevant." It was "the product of a society that could afford conservatism, a society that could solve particular social problems because there already existed a viable social structure and a general consensus on the direction of social progress." Contrary to the steadiness of U.S. society, China was confronted with large-scale crises and massive problems on all levels, social, cultural, and political—that, taken together, "negated the possibility of the general social consensus Dewey's program required."[79] Following Meinser's line of argument, Barry Keenan claims that Dewey's ideas about science, democracy, and education "fostered an elitism" in his disciples. Lamenting their "paper-tiger" status as intellectuals, Keenan writes that "they were displaced persons in a society not yet democratic, and responding superficially to their efforts to teach democracy by practicing democracy."[80] Keenan concludes that Dewey's pragmatism "offered no strategy his followers could use to affect political power."[81]

Meisner and Keenan both assume that in the early 1920s Hu was conducting "a Dewey experiment in China"—inspired by Dewey and thus automatically endorsed by him. They hold Dewey accountable for the ideas Hu promoted and fail to consider how Dewey might have diverged from Hu or even disagreed with him. Being personally familiar with Dewey, claiming to be following Dewey's ideas, and sounding very often like Dewey—all of these made Hu Shih a legitimate representative of Dewey.[82] However, in Hu's project for "the Deweyanization of China" as Lin Yu-sheng calls, the focus of pragmatism on continuous social inquiry and experimentation was turned into a justification for Hu's own cultural-intellectualism.[83] Hu took pragmatism to be a general methodology without realizing that he was actually sanctifying it as a universal doctrine. As Sor-hoon Tan points out, Hu was not sensitive enough to "treat his reformism as a hypothesis."[84] As Grieder says, "All his hopes were founded in his faith in the universal applicability of reason, and equally important, in the common aspirations of reasonable men. To admit the uniqueness of Chinese conditions would be to deny to China the expectation of redemption."[85] These are Hu's own positions that Dewey did not share—especially the dogmatic insistence on the separation of education and culture from politics.

As Lin contends, Hu's cultural-intellectualistic approach is a distinctively Chinese mode of thinking, premised on the belief that "a change of basic ideas *qua* ideas was the most fundamental change, the source of other changes." It assumes that changes in beliefs and values—namely, intellectual and cultural change—precedes and precipitates other political, social, and economic changes. As Lin elaborates:

> The cultural-intellectualistic approach was influenced by a deep-seated traditional Chinese cultural predisposition, in the form of a monistic and intellectualistic mode of thinking. It was not directly influenced by any Western sources; nor was it decisively shaped by sociopolitical conditions, which were auxiliary factors. . . . [T]his traditional mode of thinking . . . provided the source for the cultural-intellectualistic approach of the first two generations of the Chinese intelligentsia without their necessarily being conscious that their views were so derived.[86]

The political failure of the 1911 revolution confirmed Hu's deep-seated belief that "it was pointless to fashion political changes without first establishing a solid cultural foundation for the transformation of Chinese society."[87] In fact, Chen Duxiu and many other intellectuals at the time had once shared Hu's sentiment. Earlier in 1915, Chen "pleaded with his fellow intellectuals to withdraw from political life and devote themselves to educational activities and moral reform."[88] However, Chen later realized the impracticality of this approach, whereas Hu remained steadfast in his original approach.

In addition, we should bear in mind that Dewey did not publish his social and political philosophy lectures in English as Hu suggested. Dewey might not have been satisfied with them because they were too sketchy and general. They represented Dewey's ideas in the making rather than a finished product. What is of immediate relevance to our discussion here is that we should not regard these lectures as fully representing Dewey's political thought or his suggestions to the Chinese. In fact, Dewey may have reconsidered some ideas he presented in the lectures, whereas Hu seemed to hold fast to them as final answers. One significant example is the notion of progress as a retail, not wholesale, business—an idea that Hu used to advocate his own cultural reformism. Hu took this concept to heart and frequently referred to it in his own writings. In 1919 Hu stressed that the progress of human civilization is accomplished by "inches and drops."[89] In 1962 Hu recounted the story of Dewey's visit in China for the English reading public to defend Dewey—and himself—against the large-scale purging of their ideas by the Communist government in the 1950s. Hu quoted Dewey's five-stage method of thinking and claimed: "The progress of man and of society depends upon the patient and successful solution of real and concrete problems by means of active use of the intelligence of man. 'Progress,' Dewey said, 'is piecemeal. It is always a retail job, never wholesale.'"[90] Forty years later, Hu was still reiterating the point Dewey made in his 1916 essay, "Progress?"

In my view, we need to examine the context in which Dewey made the argument. At that time, Dewey was pondering the prospect of human progress in light of World War I. He was critical of the doctrine of evolution being wrongly used to support "the notion of an automatic and wholesale progress in human affairs." Such rendering of evolutionism leaves human beings with little role to play in the grand scheme of the cosmos other than to "enjoy the product of divine providence." Dewey even said that "a great and devastating war is not too great a price to pay for an awakening from such an infantile and selfish dream." As he insisted, "Progress is not automatic; it depends upon human intent and aim and upon acceptance of responsibility for its production. *It is not a wholesale matter, but a retail job,* to be contracted for and executed in sections." The essay argues that humans need to create their own history, decide their own destiny, and take full responsibility accordingly. Dewey ended by saying, "I doubt if the whole history of mankind shows any more vicious and demoralizing ethic than the recent widespread belief that each of us, as individuals and as classes, might safely and complacently devote ourselves to increasing our own possessions, material, intellectual, and artistic, because progress was inevitable anyhow." In this essay, Dewey attempted to challenge the prevailing conception of material progress as a guarantee of social progress. He argued that material prosperity was, at most, "an opportunity for progress," whose outcome depends on "deliberate human foresight and socially constructive work" (MW 10: 238).

The context of Dewey's essay in which he rendered the notion of progress "as a retail job" was quite different from the context in which Hu advocated his cultural reformism. Believing that he was being truthful to Dewey's ideas, Hu focused his piecemeal approach exclusively on attitudinal change. Even though Dewey also emphasized the importance of changing our attitudes and habits of mind to meet new challenges and demands, he knew clearly that the change in habits of mind depended on concrete changes in economic conditions and social structures. Toward the end of Hu's 1962 essay, he said, "I have brought upon my head and the head of my beloved teacher and friend, John Dewey, years of violent attack and millions of words of abuse and condemnation."[91] Little did Hu Shih know that he also would bring on Dewey the criticisms of later scholars, such as Meisner and Keenan, for prescribing and insisting on a gradualist reform approach for a society faced with the crises of social disintegration from within and imperialistic aggression from without.

In my attempt to distinguish Dewey from Hu Shih, I may have, at times, been too critical in my evaluation of Hu and his reform without acknowledging the contribution of his literary revolution, which had won him the recognition as one of the influential figures in modern Chinese history. Sor-hoon Tan's sympathetic assessment of Hu is worth noting. As she says, "Hu was promoting Dewey's philosophy while he was still developing it." Tan also argues that Hu's pragmatist work in China, his promotion of vernacular literature, was an important contribution because it made possible "the means of communication and publicity required for democracy."[92] Tan's comments were true. Even though all pragmatists would agree that pragmatism in the United States must run a different course than pragmatism in China, much remains open to argumentation and interpretation whether Hu's appropriation of Dewey was in keeping with pragmatism or was a misreading of pragmatism.[93] Despite this unresolved controversy awaiting more thorough and extensive research, we can be certain that the cultural-intellectualistic reform approach Hu adopted was his own, not Dewey's.

At the same time, we should also note that Dewey's political activism often runs a sharp contrast to Hu's conservatism. Tan was partially right when she said that Dewey and Hu Shih may have "underestimated the educative function of May Fourth political activism, which was arguably an exercise in democratic politics itself, even though it was unsuccessful in transforming China into a democratic state."[94] In fact, as demonstrated in the next chapter, Dewey may have overestimated its educative function whereas Hu Shih underestimated it. Dewey tended to be willing to consider radical changes if circumstances so required. A case in point was his support for the U.S. participation in World War I, although it "remains problematic for pragmatists."[95] In his later years, Dewey was cautious about treating revolutions or wars as the only and major method of creating drastic change. Nevertheless, Dewey was not averse to radical change per se, but to radical change through the means of violence.

Dewey remained a radical activist throughout his life—radical in the sense that he was always willing to take action and reconsider alternatives in light of changed consequences and circumstances. He was always willing, in his own words, to allow "a leeway of experimentation beyond the limits of established and sanctioned custom" (MW 12: 199). His radicalism was grounded in his faith in human intelligence to continually generate better answers to new problems. In fact, if pragmatism is to remain relevant in changing times and changing contexts, especially in today's global world with interconnected problems, pragmatism must subject its piecemeal reformism to critical scrutiny.

In one sense, Dewey exerted little influence in Hu's pragmatist experiment in China, even though Dewey was also a participant. Dewey was aware that Hu's reform approach was not very practical, that intellectual, attitudinal changes still depended on concrete changes in economic and social conditions, but Dewey was in no position to intervene. He was only a foreign guest, and he respected Hu's approach as a distinctive mode of Chinese thinking. In addition, Dewey was aware of the ideological battles between those who received overseas education in countries such as Japan, the United States, France, and Germany. Dewey acknowledged the New Culture group Hu led and was willing to "give face" to their liberal ideals. Dewey wrote to his colleague commenting on what he might have achieved in China, "My guess is that what is accomplished is mostly by way of 'giving face' to the younger liberal element. It's a sort of outside reinforcement in spite of its vagueness."[96] Dewey's particular choice of the Chinese idiom "giving face" seems to suggest that he knew that Hu was using his authority as a Western scholar to strengthen the case for his cultural-intellectualistic reform. Dewey knew that what he symbolized was more important than what he said.

When pondering whether he should stay one more year in China, Dewey wrote to his children, expressing doubts about his role in China:

> Some people say [I've] stirred up considerable interest, but when you are entirely outside the fuss interest, if any, you stir up, its about as exciting to your vanity as pouring hot water on the Arctic ice would be. [It's] much as if you were told that something you had said had aroused interest in Mars when you had never been in Mars, never expected to be there and had no share of any kind in what is doing there. I [don't] suppose I convey the idea; [it's] a curious experience, and until you've been thru [sic] a similar one you [can't] get it, for ordinarily one's vanity is a part of the reverberations—if any, and you [can't] help imagining yourself having something to do with what you are said to accomplish. But there is no more kick to this than there would be if you had a pole which happened to touch something in Marthe [sic] moon—to try once more.[97]

Dewey was puzzled by his role in China—whether he was truly a teacher or just an outsider—albeit an honored one. On another occasion, Dewey compared the difference between the Chinese and Japanese in their attitudes toward foreign experts. "When Japan engages foreign experts, she is interested in results, and so gives them a free hand till [sic] she has learned what they have to give. China engages the foreign expert—and then courteously shelves him" (MW 11: 208). Dewey seemed to be implying his own experience in China.

On the Chinese stage, Dewey played a subordinate role by supporting his students in their endeavor to reform Chinese society. As Remer pointed out in 1920, "Dewey cannot apply his own philosophy to Chinese life. It will require someone as close to Chinese thought as he is close to American thought to do this. He can, however, help this forward by his presence in China and by his advice to the Chinese who are hopeful and intelligent enough to undertake it."[98] In his attempt to estimate Dewey's influence in China, Remer made these thoughtful comments that are worth quoting in great length:

> The first impression that one gets, who tries to arrive at the Chinese estimate of Dewey, is an impression that has been cleverly connected by a Chinese university professor with the second character that is used to represent Dewey's name in Chinese. The second character means "awe-inspiring." One who talks with many Chinese about Professor Dewey long enough to get past the first statements that "Professor Dewey's thoughts are very deep," soon comes upon this feeling of awe. A whole number of the magazine, *The New Education,* was devoted to the educational and philosophical ideas of Professor Dewey. The writers, who are the most capable of any Chinese in the country to so, undertake no critical analysis of Dewey's teachings. After some search no attempt is discoverable on the part of anyone to make such a critical analysis. No one has attempted to distinguish between the ideas of Professor Dewey that was useful in China today and those that are not useful. No one has raised a voice to say that they may be harmful. But it is perhaps too soon to find any further effect than the first one. The Chinese are too polite to subject the ideas of a guest to critical analysis when he is still a guest.[99]

Remer was right that few Chinese challenged Dewey in late 1919 and early 1920. However, that the Chinese were "too polite" to subject the ideas of their guest to critical analysis was not entirely true. Clopton and Ou wrote that Dewey's influence first began to diminish after the May 30 Incident of 1925.[100] We shall see that criticisms of Dewey began to appear in newspapers in the summer of 1920, which happened while Dewey was still a guest in the country—busy traveling, lecturing, and writing. As one commentator suggests, "The only way Dewey could assist the young Chinese was to try to understand their problems from their own perspectives."[101] This is exactly what Dewey did, as we shall see in chapter four.

CHAPTER 3

THE RECEPTION OF DEWEY IN CHINA

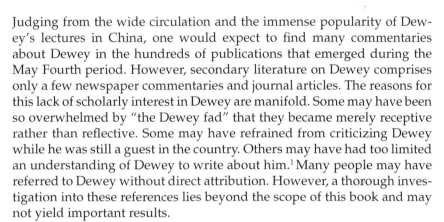

Judging from the wide circulation and the immense popularity of Dewey's lectures in China, one would expect to find many commentaries about Dewey in the hundreds of publications that emerged during the May Fourth period. However, secondary literature on Dewey comprises only a few newspaper commentaries and journal articles. The reasons for this lack of scholarly interest in Dewey are manifold. Some may have been so overwhelmed by "the Dewey fad" that they became merely receptive rather than reflective. Some may have refrained from criticizing Dewey while he was still a guest in the country. Others may have had too limited an understanding of Dewey to write about him.[1] Many people may have referred to Dewey without direct attribution. However, a thorough investigation into these references lies beyond the scope of this book and may not yield important results.

Scholars have approached the question about Dewey's influence on Chinese intellectuals through case studies. I am here concerned with how the general public received Dewey, particularly those outside the immediate circle of his associates and supporters. I attempt to piece together an impression from the archival sources collected in Beijing. The first part of this chapter analyzes newspaper commentaries about Dewey during his visit and presents a chronological account of these responses. My account features Dewey's instant success in 1919, followed by a slight decline in 1920 and 1921. The change in Dewey's popularity was affected by many things, including Bertrand Russell's visit, a growing interest among radicals in Bolshevik socialism, and the founding of the Chinese Communist Party in July 1921, coincidentally the same month when Dewey and Russell both left China. The second part of the chapter examines critical reviews of Dewey's ideas, most of which appeared after Dewey's departure. I divide my discussion into the reception of Dewey's social and political philosophy and that of his educational philosophy. My goal is to provide a dynamic picture of the cross-cultural exchange between Dewey and Chinese intellectuals during the May Fourth period.

The Dewey Fad

Thanks to the publicity efforts of Hu Shih, Dewey "became a fad" while he was in China.[2] In late March 1919, when he received Dewey's letter confirming the visit, Hu translated and published the letter in the newspaper. He also arranged a ten-day advertisement to spread the news. During the entire time Dewey was in China, his activities were closely followed in newspapers, and his lecture halls were always crowded—sometimes with as many as 3,000 people. As one Chinese observer noted, since Dewey arrived in China, every educated person was eager to hear him talk.[3] Fascinated by Dewey's lecture on experimentalism, another suggested that the government should start building scientific laboratories. He asked, "How can we cultivate the experimental spirit if we don't have well-established scientific laboratories?"[4]

One American professor who was present in China during the time mentioned Dewey's popularity in a personal letter. Seemly jealous of Dewey, this professor wrote:

> They say Dewey's lectures were dry as dinosaur bones; one chap who heard him said that if this educator should be announced to speak in the average American university, it is doubtful if fifty noses could be counted when the head of the department of education arose to announce the distinguished speaker. Not so with Chinese students. Dewey lectured in many provincial capitals. In one place there were a thousand middle-school students who did not have tickets to hear a lecture. They marched in a body to the hall, broke past the armed policemen at the door, and jammed in against the walls of an already filled hall. We might imagine a thousand American college students tramping over a squad of policemen to get out of a hall in which a two-hour lecture by this educational theorist was about to begin.

The American professor continued with the comment that somehow "Dewey's message 'took'—I'm not sure mine ever did":

> [Dewey] was very simple and down-to-earth—advocated that all education should have its "use"; that courses of study should equip a student in life to be useful as a citizen. Above all he was practical.

Students should learn by going out to life and "doing" things—learn from the doing. This made a great dent on the Chinese mind, which for centuries has been shaped by classical scholarship—exquisite reflections "about" life, yes, but from a discreet distance—life as if seen in a vista from a scholar's study, set in a templelike retreat in a pine grove on a lonely mountain. Dewey put them out in the streets.[5]

The previous examples, whether reflecting the perspective of the Chinese themselves or that of local foreigners, all attest to Dewey's fame and popularity in China.

Dewey was generally well received in Beijing where the associates and supporters of Hu Shih formed an influential liberal camp. Hu's eminent student, Lo Jialun, encapsulated Dewey's educational theories in a single sentence—school is society and education is life—which became catch phrases of the time.[6] Lo also highlighted Dewey's criticisms of exam-oriented education by saying that examinations encourage competition, make children passive, and deprive them of their self-esteem.[7] A few months later, a student at Beijing University proclaimed a "manifesto against examinations" and proudly urged his fellow students to "throw away the pen of examination," which he said was inspired by Dewey's repudiation of rote learning.[8] Such a rebellious attitude captured the overall orientation of the youth at that time. As noted, near the end of his stay, Dewey was particularly troubled by the incident in which students in Beijing jointly refused to take any examinations, insisting that they were influenced by Dewey. Dewey's decision to return to Beijing disappointed many in Guandong who were eager to hear him talk. According to the *Morning Post,* one hundred people were reported to have gathered at the train station to stop Dewey from leaving.[9]

However, during his lecture tours in various provinces of China, Dewey usually encountered strong antagonism from government and school authorities. For example, on December 24, 1919, Dewey arrived in Shandong only to discover that the governor had cabled a message to the authorities in Beijing saying, "I do not approve of their coming here to lecture, however, since they already arrived, I would cordially welcome them." This must have been an unforgettable Christmas Eve for Dewey. Moreover, at a social gathering, the minister of education in Shandong openly complained about Dewey's lecture, saying that he should have underscored the teachers' responsibility to enforce rules and regulate students' conduct.[10] Likewise, when Dewey traveled south to Nanjing and Hangzhou in the spring of 1920, the officials there were also hostile. In his lecture on "A New Conception of Life," the word "new" had to be omitted in the printing "in order not to give offense," as Dewey was notified. He told his children jokingly, "I am just as popular with the officials here as elsewhere."[11] In Hangzhou, education authorities held a private meeting with Dewey in advance to discuss the contents of his lectures. They hoped that Dewey would not say anything radical to agitate the students and that he would criticize, and thus deter, the radical behavior of students who took charge of schools and dismissed teachers.

One person, known by the pen name Boan, reported these "secret arrangements" behind the scenes and ridiculed the officials' attempt to co-opt Dewey. Boan assured that Dewey had always stood by his principles. Nonetheless, many students had begun to doubt Dewey's integrity. They believed that Dewey succumbed to the pressure from the authorities and did not truly express what he thought. Some criticized Dewey's lectures for being too vague to be useful, whereas others found them to be too simplistic and commonsensical. Some even complained that Dewey enjoyed a high standard of living and charged too much for his lectures. Boan tried to defend Dewey against these charges. He insisted that Dewey and his wife dressed rather humbly and their standard of living was not very high compared to other Westerners; Dewey's salary from the government was actually much less than what he deserved; and Dewey attempted to connect theory with practice, thereby deliberately rendering his lectures easily accessible. Boan asserted that Dewey's pragmatism was more useful than European philosophy because it focuses on concrete facts, not on abstract theories. As for the suspicion that Dewey's thoughts were "polluted by the air in Hangzhou," Boan claimed, "If you compare Dewey's own writings with the lectures, you would see no contradictions." Boan was sympathetic to Dewey because "he was truly a good and sincere person." "He came all the way to help us and enlighten us, almost forgetting that he was an American, treating us like his own fellow countrymen."[12]

By contrast, the leftist camp was hostile. Dewey was once reported to have criticized communism by saying that it cannot help with practical tasks such as river inundation and pestilence control. China should be more concerned with how to increase production effectively than with how to distribute wealth equally. One reader in a left-wing periodical, Awakening, disagreed with Dewey and said that China did not suffer as much from a shortage of special experts as from the capitalists and the bourgeois. The only thing these experts ever did was to smuggle public money into their own pockets. Even though doctors were available, ordinary people could not afford medical care and were left to die. "Isn't this the result of unfair distribution of wealth?" "Dewey has been in China for more than one year. Did he really not understand the situation of Chinese society? Or was it that the particular atmosphere in Hangzhou prevented him from expressing his true opinions?"[13]

Another reader, known by the pen name Xiping, took Dewey's criticism of Marxism's class ideology as a rejection of socialism itself and claimed that even though the number of capitalists in China was very limited, the gap between the rich and the poor was so deplorable that China absolutely needed to implement socialism.[14] Xiping was also appalled by Dewey's positive remark about the traditional family system in China: despite its many problems, the system had cultivated a sense of unity and the virtue of filial pity. In light of the fact that almost every publication at that time denounced the traditional family system and advocated drastic reform, we should be surprised that only one person challenged Dewey's opinion. In fact, Dewey did not oppose family reform, but was only concerned about some radical proposals, such as the rearing of children by public authorities.[15] Because of the weightiness of Dewey's words, his thoughtful caution was regarded as a severe threat.

In general, these left-wing critics of Dewey were concerned with the impoverished lives of the Chinese masses, as Dewey indeed was. However, they attributed the problem to the exploitation by rich capitalists and privileged officials, not to the overall lack of industrial development. Dewey thought that China's problems were "economic at root due to the struggle for existence, and that a new industrial development will in time crowd them out"—though he added that the Chinese "will take on many Western vices, and lose many of their old virtues, by carrying love of money, intrigue, mutual suspicion, and calumny into the new situation."[16] Having visited many provinces in China, Dewey was convinced that the pervasive problem of poverty should take priority over labor questions because it affected all parts of China. These commentaries on Dewey were printed in Shanghai, where the labor movement was beginning to gain momentum.[17] The critics seemed to be fervent socialists and were not satisfied with the way Dewey downplayed the struggle of labor and capital. Whereas Dewey was concerned with the development of China as a whole, they were concerned with the emerging problems in the industrializing center of China. Naturally, when Russell came to visit China with his stringent criticisms of Western capitalism and imperialism, they turned their attention to Russell. Dewey was right when he predicted that "my star such as it was will set" as the charismatic Russell arrived in China.[18]

In "My hope for Bertrand Russell," which also appeared in *Awakening*, Zhenying began by referring to Dewey and his initial popularity. However, many gradually came to think that Dewey's pragmatic sensibilities were at odds with the revolutionary spirit of the times. Even students at Beijing University became disillusioned with "the Dewey fad" and wanted to reject his influence, which was thought to reflect the defects of U.S. capitalism and religion. "Since we are disappointed in Dewey, we need to place our hope on Dr. Russell." Russell was a radical social reformer who "had learned many lessons from the [British] government and had come to complete disillusionment with it." Zhenying called

Russell an "anarchist scholar" and professed to be inspired by Russell's scholarly knowledge and his personal integrity. An apparent believer in anarchism, Zhenying anticipated that Russell's lectures would be solely on pure social philosophy—unlike what Dewey did in mixing social and political philosophy "as if humans could not survive without politics."[19]

Perhaps the best way to conclude the discussion of Dewey's reception during his stay is to look at the farewell essay one of Dewey's associates wrote on the day of his departure. "Who is Dr. Dewey?" Sun Fuyuan asked. "A synthesis of various kinds of events," he replied:

> The Dr. Dewey in your head may be the professor at the podium at Columbia University, or the person who occasionally talked to you or had lunch with you. The Dr. Dewey in someone else's head may not be the Dewey from the podium or the dinner table, because he may never meet Dewey in person. His Dr. Dewey may be the Dewey of the *Five Major Lecture Series*—the ideational Dewey, not the physical Dewey. Yet another person's Dr. Dewey may not reside in the real person or his works, but in the picture on the first page of that book. Since different people have different "Deweys" in mind, and since "Dr. Dewey" is exactly the synthesis of these different conceptions, then how does the physical Dewey that is gone today compare to this "Dr. Dewey" in our heads?[20]

Sun's seemingly scattered thoughts actually pointed to something significant: that "Dr. Dewey" was a phenomenon created by the desires, hopes, and frustrations of different individuals and groups in China. Some knew about his thoughts, and others, only his name. Sun was also right when he concluded, "Part of Dr. Dewey is not gone." An array of critical evaluations of Dewey's ideas began to appear soon after his departure.

Marxist Challenges to Dewey's Social and Political Philosophy

Strong antagonism toward capitalism and a fervent commitment to socialism characterized much of the radical thinking of the May Fourth era. Let me summarize a few major events in 1920 that contribute to the critical evaluation of Dewey's social and political philosophy. According to Arif Dirlik, Chinese radicals by 1919 had begun to "perceive the social problems of Chinese society as a local manifestation of a global capitalism that knew no boundaries."[21] However, they disagreed among themselves with regard to what form of socialism best suited China's situation and needs: anarchism, state socialism, social democracy, syndicalism, guild socialism, or Bolshevik socialism. Before 1920, anarchism had exerted a stronger influence than Marxism. However, in the spring of 1920, the Comintern sent a Russian representative, Gregory Voitinsky, to spread communist thought in China.

Responding favorably to Voitinsky, Li Dazhao established the Society for the Study of Marxist Theory in Beijing University in March 1920. In May of the same year, the Chinese Communist Party was secretly founded in Shanghai, and Chen Duxiu was elected secretary.[22] Meanwhile, Chinese intellectuals learned of the Karakhan declaration of the Soviet government, which led many to think highly of the Bolshevik regime. The declaration proposed the abrogation of all secret and unequal treaties made between the Tsarist government and China, along with a relinquishment of all its former privileges and interests without compensation. Due to these friendly acts of the Russian communists, Chinese intellectuals increasingly began to take communism seriously.[23] These events may also have created a motivation and a vocabulary to criticize Dewey's "Americanism." Even though Dewey's lectures had been very popular throughout the course of his visit, the reception of his ideas, indeed, fluctuated with these major events in 1920 and 1921. Although many still favored Anglo-American liberalism, despite the setbacks of liberal ideals at Versailles, the pro-Soviet, pro-communist tide was surely rising. Significantly, in July 1921, the month when Dewey and Russell left China, thirteen communists met in Shanghai under the supervision of two Comintern advisors to establish formally the Communist Party of China. This change in interest from U.S. liberalism to Russian communism affected the evaluation of Dewey's ideas.

The following examines three articles that evaluated Dewey's social and political philosophy: one written by Chen Duxiu in December 1919 before he was converted to communism; another by a fervent socialist, Fei Juetian, in late 1921; and the other by a prominent leader of the Chinese Communist Party, Qu Qiubai, in 1924. Even though only three sources figure in my discussion, these essays, taken together, present a clear picture of Dewey's reception—before and after Bolshevik communism was considered a more attractive model than U.S. liberalism.

Chen Duxiu was highly interested in Dewey's lecture on "Democratic Developments in America." Jerome Grieder argues that Chen's own essay, "The Basis for the Realization of Democracy," reflects a "temporary" acceptance of Dewey's suggestions for social reform.[24] At the time of writing, Chen was thinking in terms of slow reform rather than all-embracing solutions. Chen began his essay by acknowledging Dewey's broad delineation of democracy in terms of political constitution, civil rights, social equality, and economic justice. Chinese historian Benjamin Schwartz contends, "Dewey had outlined a conception of democracy which exceeded in breath and depth anything that [Chen Duxiu] understood by that term" and that Chen "accepted wholeheartedly Professor Dewey's broader conception."[25] In fact, the appeal of Dewey's conception of democracy lay not only in its "breath and depth," but also in its emphasis on social and economic issues. Chen remarked that all socialists would share Dewey's belief about social and economic democracy. Moreover, he endorsed Dewey's claim that the realization of democracy should not be limited to the political sphere. "The elevation of social life" should be the primary goal.[26] However, it was not clear whether Chen would define "the elevation of social life" in terms of open communication and free exchange of ideas as Dewey would.

Nonetheless, Chen did not accept everything Dewey said. He actually suggested that Dewey blend the four dimensions into two—the political and the socioeconomic. Chen found the analysis of democracy concerning civil rights redundant because democracy assumes that citizens are not slaves and are naturally entitled to freedom of movement, speech, publication, and religion. Moreover, Chen did not trust what Dewey said about political democracy: that individual liberties can be protected by the constitution and that public opinion can be secured by a republican government. In light of the total failure of China's republican government, Chen argued that a mere system of representation and constitutionalism would not ensure the realization of political democracy. He said that the best system was "direct legislation," which would lead to "the breaking down of the distinction between those who govern and those who were governed." People should no longer "passively allow the authority and the bureaucracy to take control; they should take the initiative in governing themselves."[27] Chen did not specify what he meant by "direct legislation." He probably meant "initiative, referendum, and recall," as Chow suggested. [28] Nevertheless, Chen, like most people at that time, clearly had little faith in any form of representative government.

Chen was especially inspired by Dewey's historical account of the United States' grassroots democracy, which was developed from self-governing villages and towns rather than imposed by the legislation of the federal government. Chen was not the only person taken with this idea. As Dewey referred in his letter, "whenever I make a remark such as the Americans do not depend upon the govt to do things for them but go ahead and do things themselves, the response is immediate and emphatic. The Chinese are socially a very democratic people and their centralized govt bores them."[29] Chen stated that he was not disheartened about the future of democracy in China because of its democratic roots in history, as manifested in various professional unions and local organizations. Democracy seemed to have failed in China because people thought of democracy in terms of constitutions imposed from above. Chen understood now that democracy must have a grassroots basis; it must penetrate into the social fabric of life; and it must begin in every town, village, and city. In Chen's view, Chinese intellectuals had been wasting their energy discussing questions such as how to organize the cabinet and the parliament, how to revise the constitution, and whether to adopt a system of centralization or federation. He lamented, "no one had cared to inquire into how people could govern and unite themselves."[30]

Few people at the time had any genuine understanding of how Western political democracy actually functioned.[31] Chen's critique of Dewey's conception of democracy reflected his own concern with socioeconomic questions as well as his limited understanding of democratic procedure and institutions. In his proposal, Chen took Dewey's advice to use China's traditional guild system to build a grassroots foundation. He believed that China could "develop democracy using England and America as a model."[32] He quoted from Dewey's lecture to emphasize democracy as the best possible society "because democracy means education. It is a tool for education. It lets you know that politics is not the special privilege of a few powerful people but is something that everyone can and should be involved in."[33] The concept of self-governance was indeed very attractive to Chen.

At the end of 1919, Chen had not considered the Marxist ideology of class struggle as a viable means for bringing about revolutionary change in China. Only later did he accept Li Dazhao's proclamation of China as a proletarian nation. Nonetheless, Chen had always been sympathetic toward the Bolsheviks and resentful of Western imperialism.[34] In light of the complexity and volatility of his own thought, it is problematic to argue for Chen's "wholehearted" acceptance of Dewey's liberalism. It is equally problematic to regard Chen's ideological orientation in late 1919 as somewhat well-defined, although temporary. As Dirlik points out, "The immediate May Fourth period in China was a period not of ideological certainty (except perhaps for liberals such as Hu Shih), but of visionary quest, ideological fluctuations, and political self-searching."[35] Chen's "temporary acceptance" of Dewey's liberalism was a case in point.

Scholars often contrast the short-lived influence of Dewey on Chen's thinking with his dramatic conversion, months later, to communism. Schwartz contends, "Democracy and Science had failed; Professor Dewey's program would require years of undramatic self-effacing work for its implementation, and even offered no hopes of any overall redemption."[36] Schwartz adds, "it would have required a 'going to the people' on the part of the intelligentsia with the aim of carrying on the political education of the people and of helping them to organize themselves along democratic lines." Chen was not ready to play this role "for which traditional Chinese civilization provided few precedents."[37] Schwartz attributes "the failure of democracy and science" to the factors in Dewey's philosophy as well as in Chen's own attitude. However, current external circumstances also played an important role in the intellectuals' growing interest in Marxism.

As Chow observes, "The appalling economic situation of China and the postwar world not only led the leftists to distrust Western political institutions, but also induced some leading liberals . . . to doubt that Western political institutions, especially representative government, were useful to cope with the existing political and economic problems both in China and in the West."[38] Likewise, Dirlik notes that after the political emergence of labor in June 1919, socialism became all the more relevant:

> The emergence of labor . . . provided seemingly incontrovertible proof that China's problems were rooted in the global forces of capitalism. The emergence of labor forced intellectuals to realize that capitalism was already a reality of Chinese society. In the postwar world, alive with the revolutionary ferment of labor against capital and of colonies against imperialist states, it seemed superfluous to distinguish social problems on the basis of national boundaries. The ideological cosmopolitanism of the New Culture Movement had predisposed intellectuals to think in universalist terms. Now socialism lost its remoteness and appeared as a universal solution as immediately relevant to China as to any other society."[39]

As Dewey also wrote, most of the young people he met in China were socialists, and "some call themselves communists."[40] In their minds, "all socialists look much alike, except that Bolsheviks are to them really carrying it out."[41] Therefore, Dewey would probably not have been too surprised to learn that many of them later indeed become communists.

In late 1921, Fei Juetian wrote a scathing critique of Dewey's lectures on social and political philosophy. Disagreeing with Dewey's comment about the cause of international conflicts, Fei claimed that conflicts exist not between nations, but between classes. It was unrealistic for Dewey to hope that through the development of industry and education, China could endow individuals with rights while also providing the opportunities to exercise those rights. This could be realized only by carrying out a revolution as the Russians did. However, Fei remarked that Dewey would be too chicken-hearted to endorse such a radical plan. Fei further asserted that Dewey's experimental approach to politics based on collective inquiry and continuous reform simply did not make sense. "If I tell the world that we should experiment with socialism and see if it works, people would think that I am crazy and would oppose this experiment. If I proclaim that socialism holds the ultimate truth to solving problems in today's society, that there is no better theory than socialism, people will become interested in its practice and help transform the theory into a reality." Fei insisted, "the experimental method would not work in reality because no one would want to risk their lives and their properties simply for the sake of experiment."[42]

Fei rejected Dewey's particularistic approach to solving social problems, claiming that social problems were all interrelated and could not be dissected into this or that particular problem. An educational problem may have been tied to a political or economic problem. The notion of a particular problem in need of a particular solution was unconvincing. Fei also disagreed with Dewey that social theories should be grounded in concrete facts, not on abstract speculations. Fei used Marx as an example to show how one ultimately needs to rely on a leap of imagination, rather than mere accumulation of facts, to diagnose social problems and offer remedies. He condemned Dewey for overly replying on contingent social knowledge at the expense of eternal truths, without which, he believed, human civilizations would not advance. He completely denounced Dewey's claim that science, with its emphasis on experimentation and facts, could be applied to solving social problems. In addition, Fei claimed that identifying problems was often more important than solving problems. For instance, autocracy had been a fundamental problem in Chinese society for thousands of years, yet no one had questioned it. Fei believed that social problems were not difficult to resolve if only the proletariat were made aware of their oppression by the capitalists and thus united to fight for their rights. He concluded that Dewey's experimental approach would not work; only a social revolution, a class war, could provide the antidote to all of China's ills.

Dewey was right when he said that China was a good place to study revolutionary idealism. As he insightfully wrote in a letter to Albert Barnes, "The whole temper among the younger generation is revolutionary, they are so sick of their old institutions that they assume any change will be for the better—the more extreme and complete the change, the better. And they seem to me to have little idea of the difficulties in the way of any constructive change." Dewey pointed out the "wonderful chance to study the psychology of revolutionary idealism—if I could only read Chinese." As Dewey also reflected, "I never realized before the meaning of the background we consciously carry around with us as a standard of criticism. Not having any such background as to modern institutions, to the liberals here anything is likely to be as true and valuable as anything else, only provided [that] it is different. The more extreme, the more likely upon the whole."[43] Fei's criticisms of Dewey, along with Dewey's own reflection, illustrate the importance of context in shaping the comprehension and application of theories.

Let me respond to the charges against Dewey's social and political philosophy. First of all, Dewey's idea of social experimentation does not mean random experimentation; it requires careful planning informed by knowledge about social realities. Dewey's rejection of metaphysical truths, independent of human intelligence and experience, does not lead to a rejection of truth per se or a denial of some universally verifiable and verified truths. Dewey's emphasis on particularity aims to avoid oversimplified abstractions and sweeping generalization that often take our attention away from concrete phenomena. It is not to suggest that social problems can be dissected into discrete units and solved separately. Dewey's emphasis on facts in guiding social inquiry is not to exclude the importance of vision but to prevent self-deluding utopianism. Evidently, Dewey's cautions fell on deaf ears to those who were longing for a deus ex machina that would lift them up from the quagmire of their shattered world.

Let us look briefly at the last piece of critique written by a committed Marxist in 1924, which expressed similar sentiments. In "Pragmatism and Revolutionary Philosophy," published in *New Youth*, Qu Qiubai stated that pragmatism in the United States was a secular philosophy aiming to maintain the status quo, not a revolutionary philosophy. When applied to China, pragmatism benefited the bourgeoisie: "It tells you how to develop your individuality and discard traditions." However, when applied to the proletariat, "it tells you not to care about socialism and just solve whatever problems you have at hand."[44] Pragmatism urged people to cope with their environment but assigned different coping mechanisms for different classes. Even though pragmatism is often associated with modern science, Qu argued that the association was erroneous because pragmatism acknowledges only practical knowledge but rejects eternal scientific truths. The fatal weakness of pragmatism was that it does not endorse the intrinsic values of theories—all theories are judged true or false simply by their consequences in practice. Pragmatists treat theories merely as tools for coping with the environment; they prize the instrumental values of theories "whose truths are valued in proportion with their usefulness."[45] In contrast to the pragmatic emphasis on "utilitarian truth," Marxism upholds scientific truths. Qu wrote, "Since we have acquired many scientific truths concerning the objective laws of the universe, we need to reconstruct society based on these scientific laws."[46] He urged his fellow Chinese not to follow the pragmatists' piece-meal approach to reform but to resort to revolution to build society anew.

One scholar observes aptly, "[Man] can adapt himself somehow to anything his imagination can cope with; but he cannot deal with Chaos. Because his characteristic function and highest asset is conception, his greatest fright is to meet what he cannot construe."[47] In a way, Chinese intellectuals, such as Chen, Fei and Qu, were all trying to make sense of what was happening to them and the world at large—particularly of what brought China to its current crises. In their desperate hope for a sweeping and all-embracing solution, they were drawn to the messianic message of Marx with its neat dualisms, simple categories, and promise of redemption. Contrary to Dewey's pragmatic outlook, Marx's and Lenin's authoritative credos found a receptive audience among the radicals such as Fei and Qu. Their criticisms of Dewey reflected the gradual consolidation of Marxist ideologies in the intellectual landscape of China.

In fact, throughout his stay, Dewey had been sympathetic to the radical's devotion to social change. He would agree with them that as one of the oldest civilizations on earth, China was in need of a "revolution." Nonetheless, it would not be a revolution in the sense of a class war that would end the misery of the poor, but in the sense of a thorough transformation of its culture and social institutions to meet modern challenges. As Dewey reflected, Marx's doctrine belongs to "compensatory psychology" and expresses "a proof of weakness." A "real revolution," Dewey thought, "will proceed from strength, from increased strength of capacity and position" (MW 12: 20). This is why Dewey urged the Chinese to use their democratic roots as a basis for the transformation of their culture and society. However, Dewey's unique vision of revolution was incomprehensible to the Chinese who were too overshadowed by the power of the West to see the light from within.

Traditionalist Responses to Dewey's Educational Philosophy

Whereas Marxist ideologies influenced the reception of Dewey's social and political philosophy, the reception of Dewey's educational philosophy was influenced by traditionalist values and beliefs. Let me briefly explain the traditionalist forces in May Fourth China to provide a framework for subsequent analyses.

During the peak of the May Fourth movement when champions of democracy and science were severely attacking Confucianism for obstructing social progress, the old intelligentsia were completely defenseless. They could not effectively defend traditional Chinese culture without a sophisticated understanding of Western civilization and its limitations. However, the situation changed when the aftermath of World War I led many to reevaluate Western thought. In his influential work, "Travel Impressions from Europe," published in mid-1920, Liang Qichao proclaimed that European civilization was bankrupt due to its blind worship of science and its overemphasis on material progress. He asserted that the spiritual tradition of China could help redress the European problem. Liang's affirmation of Chinese culture was inspired by European philosophers such as Bergson and Eucken, who were traumatized by the war and looked to the pacifist traditions in Eastern civilization for the salvation of the West. Sensitive to the self-doubts of these Western thinkers, Liang responded to their romanticized images of the East with a renewed enthusiasm about the intrinsic worth of Chinese culture. Liang told his fellow Chinese that many Western thinkers attempted to import Eastern civilization as a corrective to their own; therefore, they should endeavor to develop a new world civilization based on a synthesis of the East and the West.[48]

Following Liang Qichao's call to reconstruct traditional Chinese culture, Liang Shuming, a self-taught scholar of Indian philosophy and Confucianism, published a pioneering book in 1921, *Eastern and Western Cultures and Their Philosophies.* Liang referred to Dewey at the beginning of his book, saying that Dewey often reminded teachers and students at Beijing University that they should integrate Eastern and Western cultures for the benefit of humanity.[49] Liang was teaching Indian philosophy at Beijing University when Dewey was a visiting scholar there; therefore, Liang might have had personal contacts with Dewey. Judging from Dewey's articles about China and his philosophical orientation, what Liang said about Dewey's suggestion to harmonize Eastern and Western cultures may have been true. In his book Liang contended that the problem of the West, as revealed by the war, lay in its proclivity toward extremes. The fundamental spirit of Chinese culture—its capacity for harmonizing dualism—was especially equipped to reconcile divergent forces in the modern world and to help create a new humanistic world culture. In his attempt to defend Chinese tradition against May Fourth iconoclasm, Liang advocated the Confucian appreciation of life, the belief in moderation, the emphasis on intuition, benevolence, and contentedness. He insisted that sacrificing China's own spirit in favor of a foreign ethos would only undermine its potential and lead to self-annihilation. Apart from Liang Qichao and Liang Shuming, another group of young professors at Nanjing Normal University formed a coalition against the new literature movement led by Hu Shih. Most group members were educated in the West and were interested in classicism and Irving Babbitt's New Humanism.[50] In January 1922 they established a journal, the *Critical Review,* to disseminate their thoughts.

The first article that formally evaluated Dewey's educational theories was published in the *Critical Review.* In this article, Mo Fenglin reviewed Dewey's most well-known book, *Democracy and Education.* He first acknowledged Dewey's contribution in connecting education to broader experiences in life and the larger society. However, he criticized Dewey for neglecting religious and aesthetic dimensions of human experience. Life, he said, was not simply about coping with problems in the environment; it should also be about appreciating life itself. Because the purpose of education was to shape intellectual and moral dispositions, Dewey was wrong to talk more about geography and history than about art. Furthermore, Dewey mistook inventions for fine arts. "The intrinsic value of fine arts, such as Sophocles' and Shakespeare's plays, Phaedias' sculptures, is not to be compared to the instrumental value of an invented object such as a printing machine or a coin."[51] Art enriches life in spite of its lack of "practical" use.

Dewey's "child-centered" education was also a target of criticism. Mo accused Dewey of advocating random expressions of the impulses of youth, thus turning "the autocracy of the adult" into "an autocracy of the child." He also thought that Dewey's emphasis on interest and play would sacrifice the importance of discipline and effort in the educational process. Mo remarked that ancient sages in China set a good example of how one should overcome harsh realities and achieve excellence through strong will, rigorous discipline, and hard work. Even though Dewey's democratic theories of education successfully challenged an aristocratic style of learning enjoyed only by a privileged few, Dewey failed to consider what Mo called "natural aristocracy." These are people whose virtues and talents stand out among the ordinary and who refuse to mingle with the crowd. Influenced by Babbitt's New Humanism, Mo said that Socrates and Plato were examples of "natural aristocracy" who contributed immensely to the development of Western civilization. Dewey's theories could only apply to the education of the masses—not to exceptional people. Lastly, Mo faulted Dewey for putting too much emphasis on elementary education at the expense of adult learning. Dewey's *Democracy and Education* was, at most, a philosophy of elementary education, not a philosophy of education. Mo lamented the fact that Dewey's book was regarded as the bible of the field.

Another critic, Wu Jiangling, complimented Dewey's effort to unite knowledge with experience so that learning was not limited to what was contained in books.[52] She also perceived great value in Dewey's concept of school as a miniature society and his emphasis on learning by doing. However, Wu shared many of Mo's criticisms. She felt that Dewey's vision of education was too narrow because he talked only about controlling the environment without mentioning the importance of appreciating the environment. Wu asserted that Dewey advocated a life completely governed by rationality to the exclusion of sentiments. She also agreed with Mo that Dewey's focus on children did not qualify his book to be properly regarded as "the philosophy of education." She thought that Dewey should speak to the entire life span, rather than focusing simply on childhood. Likewise, Wu also concurred with Mo that Dewey's reliance on interest contradicted the importance of discipline and effort.

The third review, written by Lin Zhaoyin, summarized many of the objections previous critics raised. Lin criticized Dewey for emphasizing process over purpose, society over the individual, the child over the adult, interest over discipline, rationality over sentiment, participation over contemplation and practical life over spiritual life.[53] Dewey emphasized the importance of social sympathy and responsibility, but neglected the importance of individual interests and needs. In her opinion, schools should help transform society to serve individual needs better. Lin also thought that Dewey's process-oriented conception of education prevented him from specifying the aims of education, thus rendering the educational process haphazard and pointless. Like Mo, she called on ancient sages to attest to the importance of establishing profound goals in life, as opposed to moment-by-moment experimentation. She also found Dewey's scientific, rational approach to life limited and inadequate. Dewey represented a typical Western mindset in its excessive desire to control nature rather than appreciate it. Dewey "only knew the value of an active life but not that of a tranquil life."[54] Lin applauded the Indian philosopher-poet Rabindranath Tagore for promoting an ideal of tranquil life.[55]

Apart from the influence of traditionalist sentiments of the time, the education reform decree in 1922, which represented the dominance of U.S. influence on Chinese education, might have motivated these critics to evaluate Dewey's ideas on education. After 1922, people began to question foreign influences on Chinese education. In late 1924 and 1925, the movement to "restore educational sovereign rights" emerged as a response to the rise of nationalistic feelings. One critic accused U.S.-trained educators of introducing trendy theories, such as the Montessori methods or the Dalton Plan, as if they were hawking commercial goods. Classroom teachers and school principals became the real victims, constantly trying to keep up with new trends but not knowing how.[56] Another critic stated, "in the past, we relied on the ancients and now we rely on the foreigners."[57] Traditional Chinese education had prized spiritual reflection; however, the tradition had been completely discarded in the new education program. He attacked the utilitarian emphasis of the new education and deplored the fact that students of his day resisted anything that was not pleasurable and suffered greatly from lack of self-control. He faulted the students of Dewey and Paul Monroe for failing to carry out practices in keeping with their theories.[58] As pointed out in another essay, the so-called new education was American education, Japanese education, or German education—depending on where the advocates of new education received their overseas education—but not Chinese education.[59] Even though Dewey was not directly attacked in this wave of criticism, his influence and popularity dropped dramatically during these years.

In many ways, these Chinese critics' reactions to Dewey reflected a simplistic and reductionist view of pragmatism as "coping-with-the-environment-ism."[60] This was a unique nickname of pragmatism in May

Fourth China that probably owes much to Hu Shih's interpretations. In "Fundamental Ideas in Dewey's Philosophy," Hu wrote that Dewey saw experience as "methods to cope with the future, to predict the future and to relate to the future." "Experience is life," he said, and life "is the transaction between man and his environment" and "the application of thought in the guidance of all other abilities." The purpose, Hu specified, was to "utilize the environment, to conquer it, subdue it and dominate it."[61] Hu's interpretations may have led many to label pragmatism as "copying-with-the-environment-ism" as opposed to "appreciating-the-environment-ism." This label also reflected the prevailing stereotype of Westerners: they only seek to control nature, rather than to appreciate nature as it is.

Most criticisms of Dewey were misunderstandings. Take the comment for example that Dewey only talked about how individuals should contribute to the needs of society rather than how society should be transformed to fit with individual needs. It missed Dewey's central contention that education should be a vehicle for social change. Dewey's Chinese audiences were eager to throw off the shackle of tradition with all its constraints on the individual and were obviously not prepared to share his concern with "rugged individualism." Furthermore, Dewey's comments about interest and discipline often caused misunderstandings. In one sense, the Chinese critics' rejection can be seen as resulting from an inadequate understanding of what Dewey meant by interest and discipline in education. Dewey's purpose was to integrate interest and discipline into a coherent educational process without sacrificing either. He disagreed with those who assumed that interest denotes mere personal states of pleasure and that the subject matter in school has no interest for the students. Consequently, the teacher either has to present the material as sugarcoated or make the student work hard through the sheer force of will.

Disapproving of both, Dewey wrote, "To make [the subject matter] interesting by leading one to realize the connection [between school curriculum and practical life] that exists is simply good sense." However, "to make it interesting by extraneous and artificial inducements deserves all the bad names which have been applied to the doctrine of interest in education" (MW 9: 134). Dewey thought that we need to clarify what we mean by "making things interesting." In a long article, "Interest in the Relation to the Training of Will," Dewey claimed that our usual sense of the concept often signifies a "divorce of object and self." Calling the term a misnomer, Dewey remarked, "When things have to be made interesting, it is because interest itself is wanting . . . . The thing, the object, is no more interesting than it was before. The appeal is simply made to the child's love of pleasure" (EW 5: 120).

However, Dewey did not mean to suggest that all pleasures are bad. He attempted to distinguish two types of pleasure: "One is the accompaniment of activity. It is found whenever there is self-expression. It is simply the internal realization of the ongoing activity. This sort of pleasure is always absorbed in the activity itself. It has no separate existence in consciousness." The other kind of pleasure "arises from contact" and "marks receptivity." As Dewey said, "Its stimuli are external. We take interest; we get pleasure. The type of pleasure which arises from external stimulation is isolated. It exists by itself in consciousness as a pleasure, not as the pleasure of activity" (EW 5: 120). The latter is short-lived because the child's energies are divided, oscillating between moments of excitement and of boredom. The former is more enduring and educative because it stems from, and thus helps to bring, the child's existing interests and powers into richer expression and fuller development.

Having clarified Dewey's concept of interest, let us turn to his view of discipline. First and foremost, Dewey did not oppose the importance of discipline in education. His conception of discipline, however, is quite unconventional. It is by no means a form of mechanical training. As he wrote:

> A person who is trained to consider his actions, to undertake them deliberately, is in so far disciplined. Add to this ability a power to endure in an intelligently chosen course in face of distraction, confusion and difficulty, and you have the essence of discipline. Discipline means power at command; mastery of the resources available for carrying through the action undertaken. To know what one is to do and to move to do it promptly and by use of the requisite means is to be disciplined, whether we are thinking of an army or a mind. (EW 5: 120)

Discipline does not mean exerting physical efforts merely, but mental efforts as well. Because "interest is prerequisite for executive persistence," it is impossible to discipline the mind without interest. Interest and discipline thus become interconnected, not opposed.

As a matter of fact, when writing at home or lecturing in China, Dewey had to confront similar doubts and objections from those who clung to traditional methods of education and valued the function of effort in schoolwork, particularly, its moral implications. Traditionally, people believed that pure volitional effort on the part of the student, quite apart from any interest whatever, was the most desired result in school study. Dewey insisted that we should esteem highly only the effort that arises from a genuine interest in the studies themselves. Dewey found the thought absurd that a child acquires more intellectual and moral training when he conducts schoolwork with the sheer force of will, albeit unwillingly, than when he does it with complete heartfelt interest. As Dewey argued, "While the theory of effort is always holding up to us a strong, vigorous character as the outcome of its method of education, practically we do not get this character" (EW 5: 115). Instead, the outcome is often a confused soul or a dull character.

The child brought up on this basis naturally becomes accustomed to "divided attention," appearing to be occupied with the subject at hand, while secretly engaging his energies in something else. Consequently, this kind of training "reduces the person to a wishy washy, colorless being; or else to a state of moral dependence, with over-reliance upon others and with continual demand for amusement and distraction" (EW 5: 116). Dewey elaborated, "The great fallacy of the so-called effort theory is that it identifies the exercise and training of will with certain external activities and certain external results" (EW 5: 118). "I do not say that there is absolutely no moral training involved in forming these habits of external attention," Dewey wrote, but "I do say that there is a question of moral import involved in the formation of the habits of internal inattention" (EW 5: 119). In his view, "internal inattention" or "divided attention" often signifies a moral weakness rather than strength.

Dewey was not opposed to effort, but he wanted to distinguish between a normal and an abnormal sense of effort, as he did with internal and external sense of interest discussed earlier. Dewey defined normal effort as persisting through obstacles and endeavoring to transform obstacles into means for the realization of ends, whereas abnormal effort "marks simply unreal strain unnecessarily involved in any attempt to reach an end which is not part and parcel of the self's own process" (EW 5: 136). Normal effort involves "seriousness, absorption, definiteness of purpose, and results in formation of steadiness, persistent habits in the service of worthy ends." Unlike abnormal effort, it never "degenerates into drudgery, mere strain of dead lift" (EW 5: 121–22). The more genuinely interested the person is in accomplishing the goal or task at hand, the more persistent he or she will be in overcoming obstacles in the way. In this respect, effort and interest are mutually reinforcing. Unfortunately, Dewey's unique perspectives on interest and discipline/effort had often caused misunderstandings and misapplications among his detractors and followers alike.

Having compared the similarities of Dewey's reception at home and abroad, let us consider whether the embedded disparities in cultural values and social practices between Dewey and his Chinese critics might also have contributed to their criticisms. As a twentieth-century U.S. philosopher, Dewey was concerned about the meaning of democracy, the direction of social change, and the kind of education that was most appropriate for an urban, industrial society that would undergo constant changes due to scientific and technological developments. The circumstances that gave rise to Dewey's theories differed greatly from traditional education practices in China, which had been dominated by civil service examinations for 1,300 years. No critics in the United States, if I am not mistaken, ever commented that Dewey's philosophy of education should be merely regarded as a philosophy of elementary education. The Chinese critics evidently missed Dewey's concept of education as a continuous process of lifelong learning and renewed experiences. As Dewey wrote in *Democracy and Education:*

> Normal child and normal adult . . . are engaged in growing. The difference between them is not the difference between growth and no growth, but between the modes of growth appropriate to different conditions. With respect to the development of powers devoted to coping with specific scientific and economic problems we may say the child should be growing in manhood. With respect to sympathetic curiosity, unbiased responsiveness, and openness of mind, we may say that the adult should be growing in childlikeness. One statement is as true as the other. (MW 9: 55)

Even though one can use Dewey's words to refute quickly this "Chinese" criticism as erroneous, Dewey himself would want to understand these critics' perspective before he made any judgment. If we try to conceptualize education from the Chinese perspective, we could find that this misinterpretation resulted from differences in cultural beliefs and practices.

Chinese intellectuals tended to equate education with higher learning due to the dominance of civil service examinations in the history of education in China. Even though the practice was abolished in 1905, these critics were still influenced by the traditional views of education. In his 1922 essay, "What is New Education?" Chen Duxiu summarized traditional conceptions of education as follows: it was characterized by the system of civil service examinations and the study of moral teachings and classics, the goal of which was for individuals to aspire to be a sage or an exemplary person in society. New education, Chen said, was characterized by the school system and the study of sciences, the goal of which was to transform society. Chen labeled the old approach to education as "individualistic" and "didactic," whereas the new approach was "social" and "inspirational."[62] Chen's comments help us understand why Chinese critics of Dewey frequently called on ancient sages to attest to what they deemed as loftier aims of education.[63]

Due to the demand of civil service examinations, discipline and effort were regarded as quintessential educational virtues. To prepare for these exams, the candidates were required to memorize the Four Books and Five Classics. These texts amounted to 400,000 words in total, which alone would take an average of six years to memorize if the candidates could memorize 200 words a day, not to mention that they needed to study the secondary literature on these canonical works.[64] One story in the history of civil service examinations may help illustrate why discipline and effort were so highly valued. The oldest person to have obtained the highest degree was a man who had tried and failed many times in his life but finally succeeded at age ninety-eight.[65] He was not assigned a government position because of his age, but he was awarded an honorary statue. In fact, the centuries-old belief in effort persists even today. Contemporary research on the "learning gap" between Asian and U.S. students has shown that the educational success of Asian students can largely be attributed to their belief in the role of effort in achievement, in contrast to the American emphasis on innate abilities.[66]

Despite their political biases or cultural misunderstandings, these Chinese critics did point out one thing that was not in the foreground of Dewey's philosophy of education, that is, concrete references to aesthetic experiences and spiritual values in life. Aesthetics was a subject that Dewey did not address systematically until the 1930s. Because of this limitation, Dewey was also challenged by his critics in the United States, first by Randolph Bourne in the late 1910s and later by Lewis Mumford in 1926. In "Twilight of Idols," Bourne said that although Dewey "always meant his philosophy, when taken as a philosophy of life, to start with values. But there was always that unhappy ambiguity in his doctrine as to just how values were created." Without "the vividest kind of poetic vision," Dewey's instrumentalism made it easy to "assume that just any growth was justified and almost any activity valuable so long as it achieved ends."[67]

Following Bourne's line of argument, Mumford accused Dewey of having "little to say about art, and when he did consider it, he failed to see anything other than its instrumental value and consequently missed its essence. He did not realize that inventions and fine arts were different." Mumford challenged Dewey's "pragmatic acquiescence" to "the dominance in American culture of the utilitarian type of personality." Interestingly, the criticism Dewey received from his Chinese critics—that he focused too much on the external environment while neglecting the power for internal transcendence—seemed to correspond with Mumford's comment when he argued that "man need not accommodate himself pragmatically to external circumstance, for he had the capacity to act creatively, as an artist, to shape the aims and necessities of his world."[68]

Dewey later developed the notion of consummatory, aesthetic experience perhaps as a response to his critics in the United States. He may also have been motivated by a personal desire, as he told Sidney Hook, to "get into a field I haven't treated systematically." Dewey's critics in China and the United States both pointed to an area of Dewey's thinking that required more elaboration if, to use Westbrook's words, "the 'other' Dewey 'reaching out to wider sources of experience' was to be more apparent to his readers." Indeed, Dewey needed to "say more about life's consummations if he was ever to escape the charge that his was a philosophy that left its readers all dressed up with no place to go."[69]

Reconsidering "The Dewey Experiment"

One additional point about Dewey's reception and his role in China is worth noting. Even though Chinese intellectuals seemed to have easy access to the articles Dewey wrote about China for readers in the United States, only two of them had ever been translated into Chinese and made available to the public. One was Dewey's essay on "New Culture in China," printed in the *Morning Post*—apparently by someone from the liberal camp, although the name of the translator was not reported.[70] In this essay, Dewey started by describing the positive aspects of the New Culture movement, saying that it was governed by the belief that "the real supremacy of the West is based, not on anything specifically Western, to be borrowed and imitated, but on something universal, a method of investigation and of the testing of knowledge" (MW 13: 110). However, toward the end of the article he stated, "Chinese educated youth cannot permanently forswear their interest in direct political action," and "their attention needs to be devoted more than it has been detailed, to practical economic questions, to currency reform, public finance and problems of taxation, to foreign loans and the Consortium" (MW 13: 119). Importantly, we should note that this article was not translated in its entirety. Only the first half of the article, which contained favorable comments about the movement, was translated and published in the newspaper on four consecutive days. The translator stopped short of translating the other half, which contained Dewey's critical comment I just quoted.

The other Dewey article translated into Chinese was on Chinese philosophy of life, printed in a journal that promoted Chinese culture and literature.[71] In this article, "As the Chinese Think," Dewey expressed admiration for traditional Chinese culture. He wrote, "industrialism as it exists in the western world is a menace to what is deepest and best in Chinese culture," and "the Chinese philosophy of life embodies a profoundly valuable contribution to human culture and one of which a hurried, impatient, over-busied and anxious West is infinitely in need" (MW 13: 223). The reason why only these two articles were selected seems clear: they could be used to support an intellectual movement—the New Culture movement and neotraditionalism respectively.

With these, I would like to return to the assumption about "the Dewey experiment" in China. The phrase was used to depict a phenomenon in which Dewey's Chinese disciples experimented with his ideas to see if they would work in the Chinese context. However, this experiment seemed to have somehow extended beyond Dewey's disciples to encompass a wide array of individuals and groups who used Dewey to validate their own thoughts. They experimented with Dewey in light of their own conflicting desires. They shared many things in common: frustration with political corruption, fear of national extinction, and hope for a new social order. Most important, they all seemed to face an internal contradiction between staying Chinese and becoming modern—and Western. However, they disagreed among themselves with regard to which road would lead China to freedom and authenticity. The conflicting views and images of Dewey as we have seen in the previous discussion were the result of these contending ideologies and emotions.

Against the backdrop of the chaotic May Fourth China, one thing seems clear: Dewey meant different things to different people—depending on what purposes their particular versions of Dewey served and what part of Dewey's thoughts they could use to support certain claims. For instance, Hu Shih's Dewey was one who emphasized the scientific method and insisted on a nonpolitical, gradualist approach to reform. Chen Duxiu's Dewey was one who acknowledged the importance of socioeconomic democracy over political democracy. Liang Shuming's Dewey was one who advocated the merger of Eastern and Western cultures to create a new world culture. In the eyes of the students, Dewey was one who inspired their protest against examinations. In the eyes of the officials, Dewey was a bad influence on students. Indeed, Dewey and his theories were used differently by different people. In one sense, we may accept the assumption about "the Dewey experiment," although granted, "Dewey" himself was being experimented on. In another sense, we may also argue that there was, indeed, a Dewey experiment going on in China—one that Dewey himself was conducting. He was testing whether Western conceptions about Chinese politics, social psychology, and cultural beliefs reflected Chinese realities or Western prejudices. He was determined to present Chinese ways of life and habits of mind from their own perspectives, hoping thus to find "some way of cooperation for common ends" between the East and the West (MW 13: 218). With this, let us turn to the next chapter on Dewey as a learner in China.

CHAPTER 4

DEWEY AS A LEARNER

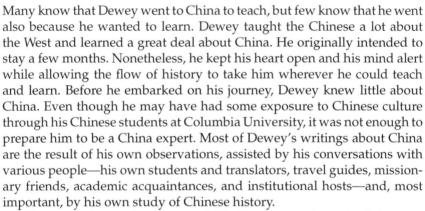

Many know that Dewey went to China to teach, but few know that he went also because he wanted to learn. Dewey taught the Chinese a lot about the West and learned a great deal about China. He originally intended to stay a few months. Nonetheless, he kept his heart open and his mind alert while allowing the flow of history to take him wherever he could teach and learn. Before he embarked on his journey, Dewey knew little about China. Even though he may have had some exposure to Chinese culture through his Chinese students at Columbia University, it was not enough to prepare him to be a China expert. Most of Dewey's writings about China are the result of his own observations, assisted by his conversations with various people—his own students and translators, travel guides, missionary friends, academic acquaintances, and institutional hosts—and, most important, by his own study of Chinese history.

However, those who have read *The Dewey Experiment in China* may have the impression that Dewey often parroted the views of Hu Shih in his own writings about China. Keenan asserts, "Dewey was a good student in reporting what they [his disciples] said."[1] Because Dewey did not know the language, we could easily assume that he could not form his own judgments. In fact, Dewey's own independent thinking will be all the more apparent when we consider how his views about the May Fourth movement differed from those of Hu Shih. In his long sojourn, Dewey learned about the Chinese social psychology and philosophy of life. At the same time, he also came to understand the West and to question its Eurocentric worldviews. This chapter weaves a new theme into the old tale about Dewey's visit to China, namely, his own education. The following discusses Dewey's learning experiences from the perspectives of his role as a political commentator, a goodwill ambassador, and a cultural anthropologist, concluding with the meaning of Dewey's trip in the larger context of his life and work.

Dewey as a Political Commentator

As noted, Dewey arrived in China three days before the outbreak of the May Fourth movement. His timely presence provided a great opportunity for his own learning, giving him a vantage point to witness the unfolding of the event. It also put him in a unique position to serve as a political commentator for the *New Republic*.

Let me recount the event briefly. On May 4, 1919, 3,000 students in Beijing held a mass demonstration against Japanese imperialism and domestic political corruption. In big cities, general strikes supporting the students ensued along with large-scale boycotts against Japanese goods. This series of events following the student demonstration led Dewey to remark, "Talk about the secretive and wily East. Compared, say, with Europe, they hand information out to you on a platter . . . and sandbag you with it."[2] Impressed by the outpouring of public support for these student-initiated activities, he wrote to his children, "To think of kids in our country from fourteen on, taking the lead in starting a big cleanup reform politics movement and shaming merchants and professional men into joining them. This is sure some country."[3] In "The Student Revolt in China," Dewey interpreted the event for his U.S. readers saying, "The possibilities of organization independent of government, but capable in the end of controlling government, have been demonstrated." Dewey felt so hopeful that he even predicted, "It would be highly surprising if a new constitutionalist movement were not set going. The combination of students and merchants that has proved so effective will hardly be allowed to become a mere memory" (MW 11: 190). To Dewey, these events embodied the power of public opinion. As he later indicated, "the most impressive single feature of my stay in China was witnessing the sure and rapid growth of an enlightened and progressive public opinion" (MW 13: 147). This experience was reassuring to Dewey because he had always believed that public opinion as a moral and intellectual force should and would triumph over the forces of coercion and violence.

Such an eye-opening experience was not unprecedented for Dewey. Earlier in his life when Dewey was moving from rural Michigan to Chicago in 1894, he found himself in the midst of the Pullman Strike.[4] He was so excited about the scene that he wrote to his wife, Alice, "Every conceivable thing solicits you; the town seems filled with problems holding out their hands and asking somebody to solve them—or else dump them in the lake. I had no conception that things could be so much more phenomenal and objective than they are in a country village, and simply stick themselves at you, instead of leaving you to think about them.[5] The strike and chaos Dewey witnessed in Chicago uplifted rather than dampened his spirit. He understood them as a necessary condition for realizing industrial democracy. The burning of a few freight cars was "a cheap price to pay . . . to get the social organism thinking." However, the hostility of "higher class" intellectuals toward the "lower class" workers was "so hopeless and discouraging" to him that he remarked, "Professional people are probably worse than the capitalists themselves."[6] Despite the strike's eventual defeat by the government's armed forces, Dewey believed that it succeeded in stirring public attention and discussion. As Westbrook points out, "Dewey was prone throughout his life to such hopeful predictions of the unintended consequences of the defeat of democratic reform," and "such efforts at prophesy are a telling index to his own political desires." Westbrook is also right when he says, "Dewey's record as a prophet was undistinguished."[7] Nonetheless, one can still find insight in a prophecy that was not fulfilled.

Some interesting similarities between the Pullman Strike and the Chinese student demonstration are worth noting. They bring Dewey's political activism and radical impulses into fresher relief. Dewey was as sympathetic to the workers as he was to the students. His Chicago colleagues' disapproval of the strike correlated with Hu Shih's negative opinion about the student revolt. Hu insisted that the students should devote themselves to their studies rather than to politics; Dewey, on the contrary, endorsed the students' revolt as a gesture of righteous indignation.[8] He interpreted their voluntary action as embodying "the awakening of China from a state of passive waiting" (MW 11: 187) and as "showing what educated China can do, and will do, in the future" (MW 11: 191). Dewey was glad for young China because it now realized, or so it seemed to him, that it did not need to be saved from without. Nonetheless, Dewey knew that merely resorting to protests and rebellions would not bring about constructive change. He concluded with this hypothetical remark, "If the present organization persists and is patiently employed for constructive purposes, then the fourth of May, nineteen hundred and nineteen, will be marked as the dawn of a new day. This is a large if. But just now the future of China so far as it depends upon China hangs on that If" (MW 11: 191).

Six months later, Dewey's hope that the impact of the student movement would effect significant political change had been disappointed. Dewey and Alice seemed to have anticipated that the movement would lead to political revolution.[9] However, it did not accomplish much other than preventing China's signing of the Versailles peace treaty. In "The Sequel of the Student Revolt," Dewey said retrospectively that the "relative political failure" was due to "the youth and inexperience of the students," "the fear of excess," "the difficulty in maintaining continuous organized cooperation with the mercantile guilds," and "the natural waning of enthusiasm when [the] crisis was past" (MW 12: 23). However, it was a mistake, as Dewey reminded, to think that the movement proved to be of no avail. The significance of the movement lay in its intellectual implications. "It was the manifestation of a new consciousness, an intellectual awakening in the young men and young women who through their schooling had been aroused to the necessity of a new order of belief, a new method of thinking" (MW 12: 27). The students believed that the new method of thinking should be imported from the West, as they began to realize that the the power of the West resided not in its battleships but in its ideas.

The raising of a new intellectual awareness, often identified as the New Culture movement, was greatly facilitated by the explosion of the publishing industry, where discussion of social questions was predominant. In the new press, all kinds of Western social and political theories were translated and discussed, including anarchism, liberalism, socialism, Marxism, and of course, Dewey's own pragmatism. In the intellectual marketplace of ideas, any goods would be favored as long as they had Western packaging. Even though Dewey questioned the students' interest in Marxism, he acknowledged their overall intellectual enthusiasm and said, "in a country where belief has been both authoritatively dogmatic and complacent, the rage for questioning is the omen of a new epoch." Nonetheless, Dewey was aware that their apparent zeal for Western learning did not reflect a pure interest in the ideas themselves, but rather "a desire for such knowledge of them as will facilitate discussion and criticism of typical Chinese creeds and institutions" (MW 12: 26).

In "New Culture in China," Dewey explicitly said that the New Culture movement, with its exclusive attempt at cultural reform, "was in its deeper aspect a protest against all politicians and against all further reliance upon politics as a direct means of social reform." He said, "this anti-political bias" was being firmly established and "becoming more and more characteristically Chinese." As he noted, "the belief that reform is conditional upon scientific and social changes, is in a way a return to Chinese modes of thinking, a recovery of an old Chinese idea, plus an assertion that the power of that idea was not exhausted and terminated by Confucianism" (MW 13: 110–11). Another feature that characterized May Fourth China, apart from the belief that reform in culture was an antecedent of other reforms, was a rising demand for Chinese leadership due to nationalistic feelings.

However, he noticed a contradiction in the call for Chinese leadership and the rejection of China's Confucian past. Dewey asked, "How can reversion to Chinese leadership coincide with attack upon Chinese customs and habits of mind? How can it coincide with a realization that the real source of Western superiority is found, not in external technique, but in intellectual and moral matters?" (MW 13: 111). May Fourth China was, indeed, marked by contradictory aspirations. Dewey commented, "history is never logical, and many movements are practically effectual in proportion to their logical inconsistency." Nonetheless, he had no doubt that "the idea of the supremacy of intellectual and moral factors over all others is itself a native Chinese idea" (MW 13: 114). Even though Dewey recognized the importance of cultural reform, he had doubts about such a single-minded approach. Unlike these Chinese intellectuals, Dewey did not establish an arbitrary dualism between cultural and political reform. The pragmatic Dewey knew that constructive social change depends on practical and political means.

Even though Dewey acknowledged the importance of Western learning, he sensed a more pressing need for China to develop her industry. His extensive travels to eleven provinces allowed him to encounter the lives of the masses firsthand, and he was convinced that China's poverty and industrial backwardness should be a top priority. In light of the history of democratic development in the West, Dewey believed that people's thinking would change along with the changes in their daily lives. Dewey thought that Chinese intellectuals were too preoccupied with absorbing new thoughts and new theories to accomplish any effective political or practical change. As Dewey observed, they "have no material to work upon even [if] they wanted to start a practical movement" and "are still too theoretical to engage successfully in practical movements."[10] According to Alice, Dewey had attempted to guide the young intellectuals toward more practical paths. In one of his lectures in southern China, he told them, "it was not theories [about socialism] and free thought and free [love] that China needed, it was teaching the people how to improve agriculture and cotton and silk and more especially their own lives." In the same letter to their family, Alice revealed that the students complained that Dewey's lectures were "not intellectual enough." "Think how China has [changed] Pa" was her reaction to this criticism.[11] Perhaps China had made Dewey less "intellectual" because the Chinese equated "the intellectual' with pursuing book knowledge rather than solving practical problems.

Dewey's dream for a true political revolution following the May Fourth student demonstration did not materialize. However, one still finds great insights in Dewey's writings about China, despite his unfulfilled prophecies.[12] For instance, Dewey understood that the salvation of China depended not so much on the few intellectuals in the cities as on the ordinary men and women throughout China. As Dewey evaluated the New Culture movement led by his Chinese disciples, he said:

There are hours when, stimulated by contact with what is best in the movement, I am willing to predict that it will succeed and, in succeeding with its own problems, will also give to the world things of new and permanent value. There are other times, when, after contact with the darker features of the situation, I wonder that the supporters of the cause do not all lose hope and pessimistically surrender. It is easy to see why some give up effort and devote themselves to making the best of a bad situation by feathering their own nests. At the end, one comes back to the sobriety, the industry, the fundamental solidity of the average common man. These qualities have weathered many previous storms. They will pull China through this one if they are redirected according to the demands and conditions of that modern world that has thrust itself so irresistibly and so disturbingly upon China. The [N]ew [C]ulture movement is a significant phase of the attempt to supply the direction so profoundly needed. (MW 13: 120)

Dewey's expectations for his disciples were not realized, but he was insightful in placing his ultimate hope on "the average common man." History shows that in the end the masses pulled China through its troubles. Unfortunately, his disciple Hu and his group of culture reformers did not succeed in supplying the needed direction because their elitist tendencies ultimately isolated them from the masses. The radical and politically minded Marxists knew how to mobilize the masses and to awaken them from their long slumber.

Dewey as a Goodwill Ambassador

Although Dewey's stay in China was a rare opportunity for him to gain an insider perspective on the conditions of the Far East, it also entailed a moral responsibility. His Chinese audiences sometimes asked Dewey during his lectures to respond to the Versailles Peace Conference. The most frequently asked question, as Dewey put it, amounted to this: "Since the decision of the peace conference shows that between nations might still makes right, that the strong nation gets its own way against a weak nation, is it not necessary for China to take steps to develop military power, and for this purpose should not military training be made a regular part of its educational system?" (MW 11: 180). Whether Dewey provided a satisfying answer to this difficult question is not known; however, he heard these concerns and took them seriously. Throughout the course of Dewey's writing about China, one senses Dewey's ongoing concern about the role of the United States in the Far East. Like his views on the May Fourth movement, Dewey's suggestions for U.S. diplomacy in China also underwent significant changes.

Early in his stay, Dewey noted a pro-American sentiment, especially prevailing in the intellectual circles of China. In the eyes of many Chinese, Japan was the despoiler, whereas the United States was the rescuer. Resentment toward Japan had contributed to a "pathetic affection for America." As Dewey stated in "The International Duel in China," "China in her despair has created an image of a powerful democratic, peace-loving America, devoted to securing international right and justice, especially for weak nations." He insisted that China's idealization of the United States should impose "humility rather than self-glorification upon Americans" (MW 11: 196). Even though he applauded the American influence "in the educational line," he cautioned that "this success is not of a kind to be impressive when it comes to determination of international affairs" (MW 11: 231).

The key to peace in the Far East, Dewey claimed, lay in the relationship between Japan and the United States. In his own writings, Dewey tried to influence U.S. policy toward China by attacking Japanese propaganda. He urged U.S. politicians not to be bought off by Japan or be taken in by their liberal posturing. He wrote:

> Americans may sometimes wonder in a perplexed way about the contrary reports and views of travelers in the Far East and conclude that the latter become pro- or anti-Japanese for temperamental or accidental reasons. Here is the explanation. Those who have not gone further than Japan realize Japan as a fact; the continent is still a place on the map, an impersonal factor in an intellectual calculation. Those who with eyes and ears half-open have stayed upon the continent realize the condition which has been created by Japanese [propagandist] methods. (MW 13: 81–82)

Before Dewey went to the Far East, he had little idea of Japan's actual intention to colonize China, hidden within its eager pursuit of economic interests. Immediately on his departure from Japan and arrival in China, he sensed the significance of differences perceived in the two countries. After learning more about the status of Japan in international politics and its predatory attitude toward China, Dewey perceived the seed of a future war being deeply planted in China. He cautioned U.S. readers, "every appeal to American sympathy on the ground of the growing liberalism of Japan should meet with neither credulity nor cynicism, but with a request to know what this liberalism is doing, especially what it is doing about China and Siberia" (MW 13: 84). When commenting on the greed of Japanese businessmen and the aggression of Japanese militarists, Dewey said, "it is no pleasure for one with many warm friends in Japan, who has a great admiration for the Japanese people as distinct from the ruling military and bureaucratic class, to report such facts"

(MW 12: 33). Despite this caveat, Dewey knew that he needed expose these facts to enlighten public opinion.

Apart from informing U.S. readers of the reality of Japanese imperialism, Dewey also gave suggestions concerning what the United States should do to help China overcome its current crisis and to embark on the path of normal development. In his earlier writings, Dewey asked the United States to "sympathetically comprehend the Chinese situation," to be "patient and persistent" in its foreign policies (MW 11: 226–27), and to realize "the enormous power which is now in her hands" (MW 11: 198). Dewey advised that the U.S. government assist China in important practical tasks such as improving agriculture, constructing railways and inland waterway systems, and regulating currency systems. He hoped that such potential on the part of the United States would not be "thrown away by reason of stupidity and ignorance" (MW 11: 198). To ensure that China be made "the mistress of her own economic destinies," Dewey stressed that these large-scale tasks should be performed by "enlisting the cooperation of Chinese voluntaryism" and that U.S.-trained Chinese students should administer the implementation of these plans (MW 11: 243). Dewey was certain that when these tasks were accomplished, China should be able to take care of itself politically.

Because Dewey knew that the masses of Chinese people were relying on the United States for their redemption, he found the policy of "no foreign entanglements" deplorable. He traced the root of the United States' national egotism to the fear that engagement with the undemocratic world would threaten its internal democracy (MW 12: 5). In an unusually scathing tone, he remarked, "the contrast between prior professions and actual deeds was so obvious as to evoke revulsion" (MW 12: 3). Dewey's sense of obligation as a close witness of China's predicaments and his deep convictions about the interconnectedness of international affairs propelled him initially to espouse an activist, paternalistic approach toward China. However, as his understanding of Chinese history, culture, and psychology deepened, his initial activism mellowed. In his response to whether the United States should join the alliance with Great Britain to resolve the crisis in the Far East, Dewey said, "There is an obligation upon us not to engage too much or too readily with them until there is assurance that we shall not make ourselves worse" (MW 12: 7). Experience had taught him much about the dark realities of international politics: professed ideals for democracy and peace could turn out to serve imperialistic ends.

The shift in Dewey's thinking was most evident in an article written shortly after his return as a response to the upcoming Pacific Conference in Washington. In "Federalism in China," Dewey advised against exogenous intervention in China's domestic affairs and suggested instead a "hands-off" policy:

The hope of the world's peace, as well as China's freedom, lies in adhering to a policy of Hands Off. Give China a chance. Give her time. The danger lies in being in a hurry, in impatience, possibly in the desire of Americans to show that we are a power in international affairs and that we too have a positive foreign policy. And a benevolent policy from without, instead of promoting her aspirations from within, may in the end do China about as much harm as a policy conceived in malevolence. (MW 13: 155)

Dewey's earlier paternalistic impulses gave way to a deep respect for the self-determination and self-government of the Chinese people. His earlier enthusiasm gave way to a healthy skepticism that kept him suspicious of any proposal to place China under international tutelage.

Importantly, we should note that Dewey's proposal for a hands-off policy not be labeled as "isolationist" because "nonintervention" did not mean noncommunication or noninteraction. Allan Ryan's comment that Dewey "took up the isolationist and Outlawry of War banner" after he returned to the United States did not do justice to Dewey.[13] Dewey's noninterventionist approach was the result not of cold indifference, but of a profound respect for China's capacity for self-governance. Dewey realized that "China will not be saved from outside herself" because she "is used to taking time for her problems: she can neither understand nor profit by the impatient methods of the western world which are profoundly alien to her genius." Transformation from within was the only hope, and the United States could best help China by making sure that she "gets the time she needs in order to effect this transformation, whether or not we like [the] particular form it assumes at any particular time" (MW 13: 171). Treating China like "a sick patient rather than an active living force" would only weaken her and paralyze her (MW 13: 182). Even though a policy of nonintervention "may not seem benevolent," he said, "I do not believe that any nation at present is wise enough or good enough to act upon the assumption of altruism and benevolence toward other nations" (MW 15: 187).

In "America and the Far East," written a few years after his return, Dewey reiterated his opposition to the paternal attitude of the United States in its interaction with China, particularly in light of the increasing resentment toward missionary efforts in China. He wrote:

We have gone there with ideas and ideals, with sentiments and aspirations; we have presented a certain type of culture to China as a model to be imitated. As far as we have gone at all, we have gone in loco parentis, with advice, with instruction, with example and and precept. Like a good parent we would have brought up China in the way in which she should go. There is a genial and generous aspect to all this. But nonetheless it has created a situation, and that situation is fraught with danger. (LW 2: 174)

The danger lay in the resentment on the part of the Chinese toward the "the air of superiority" foreign guardians, such as American missionaries, assumed and in the consequent charges on the part of the foreign helpers that the Chinese were ungrateful. Dewey urged the United States to alter its "traditional parental attitude, colored as it has been by a temper of patronage, conscious or unconscious, into one of respect and esteem for a cultural equal" (LW 2:175). Throughout the course of his stay in China and the immediate years following his return to the United States, Dewey devoted much thinking to finding out what America should, or should not, do to contribute to peace and prosperity in that region. Without a doubt, Dewey's views underwent significant, if not dramatic, changes. To understand and appreciate Dewey's growing sensitivity, openness, and farsightedness as reflected in his final proposal for a hands-off policy in China, we need to examine closely the process by which Dewey learned to understand and respect China on its own terms.

Dewey as a Cultural Anthropologist

One major purpose of Dewey's trip to the Far East was to "get some acquaintance" with what was happening on the other side of the world. Soon after he arrived, he became interested in more than collecting exotic stories that might impress his grandchildren. His mind was set on an intelligent inquiry into China's predicaments, and his heart, on the destiny of its people. Obviously, understanding an old civilization and the causes of its current crises was not an easy task. As Dewey admitted to a close friend, "[It's] an absurdly pretentious performance in one way, with my short stay here and no knowledge of the language" to write "on the general political and social psychology of the Chinese as affecting the [present] situation." However, Dewey thought, "it will be just as good as most of the stuff travelers put out [for] the American reader, and a little better than some for it will give some attempt at interpretation from the Chinese [viewpoint]."[14]

As a reflective thinker, Dewey soon realized that grave misunderstandings characterized the history of contact between the West and China. The reason was that many of the political and economic conceptions of the Western world did not apply to Chinese situations. In other words, Dewey was realizing that a non-Eurocentric point of view—a concept alien to Dewey's time but quite in keeping with his pragmatic sensibility—was key to an accurate and sympathetic understanding of China. Dewey summarized this unusual cultural experience to a former student of philosophy: "This is really 'the other side of the world' in every sense, and it [is] most interesting to see a culture where so many of our prepossessions are reversed. It has a tendency to make academic affairs including [academic] philosophy shrink. [It's] a good thing we [can't] [visit] the rest of the universe in space; our [own] habits and beliefs would shrink too much."[15] On another occasion, Dewey wrote, "The visitor spends his time learning, if he learns anything about China, not to think of what he sees in terms of the ideas he uses as a matter of course at home." For Dewey, the need to cultivate a culturally sensitive perspective is what gave China its "overpowering intellectual interest for an observer of the affairs of humanity" (MW 13: 75). Given that the Western worldview in the early twentieth century was predominantly Eurocentric, one finds remarkable intellectual farsightedness and open-mindedness in Dewey's reflections on the problem of Eurocentrism. A tyro in Chinese history, Dewey inevitably made a few mistakes in his judgments about current events, but he was quick to correct them and continued to learn along the way.

One of Dewey's misjudgments pertains to his overzealous attitude toward the student movement, which was largely grounded in his own political desires. As mentioned earlier, Dewey was fascinated by the power of public opinion and grassroots activism demonstrated in the student movement. His spontaneous enthusiasm kept him, as he put it, "always on the alert to see what is coming next," despite the attempt "to repress one's desire for a [little] more [direct] western energy to tackle things before they get to the toppling over point."[16] However, everything seemed to have returned to normalcy after a few weeks of heated agitation, leaving Dewey's high hopes for significant change unfulfilled. The disappointed Dewey sometimes found the ingrained passivity of the Chinese people baffling. As Dewey wrote to his children one month after the outbreak of the student demonstration: "Status quo is China's middle name, most status and a little quo. I have one more motto to add to 'You Never Can Tell' and 'Let George Do It.' It is, 'That is very bad.' Instead of concealing things, they expose all their weak and bad points very freely, and after setting them forth most calmly and objectively, say 'That is very bad.'"[17] Dewey observed that the Chinese "talk more easily than they act—especially in politics," and they love "finding substitutes for positive action, of avoiding entering upon a course of action which might be irrevocable" (MW 11: 175–76). Dewey later came to realize that "China has never been anything but apathetic towards governmental questions. The student revolt marked a temporary exception only in appearance" (MW 12: 24). Implying his own error, Dewey wrote, "The new comer [*sic*] in China in observing and judging usually makes the mistake of attaching too much significance to current happenings" (MW 13: 149). He even remarked in a tongue-in-cheek manner, "After a few months in China, a visitor will take an oath, if he is wise, never to indulge in prediction" (MW 13: 120). Refraining from making predictions may be easy for others but difficult for Dewey, whose "lifelong project" is to "intelligize practice" by anticipating consequences and applying foresight.[18] Dewey still allowed himself to make a few more predictions in his later articles on China, but a few more in Dewey's eyes probably would not count as indulgence.

On one occasion, Dewey posed the question, "Is it possible for a Westerner to understand Chinese political psychology?" He quickly answered, "certainly not without a prior knowledge of the historic customs and institutions of China, for institutions have shaped the mental habits, not the mind the social habits" (MW 13: 215). As a committed and diligent learner about China, Dewey read Chinese history; he also read local English newspapers to keep abreast of the latest political developments; he shared and exchanged views with local foreigners; and he even took Chinese language lessons from a tutor. Dewey could have made the same comment as his wife when she said, "Since reading of their history I can see why they have always been in a state much like this."[19] Dewey's exposure to Chinese history, coupled with his own observations, led him to remark: "China can be understood only in terms of the institutions and ideas which have been worked out in its own historical evolution" (MW 11: 216).

To be more specific, Chinese politics "has to be understood in terms of itself, not translated over into the classification of an alien political morphology" (MW 11: 211). According to Dewey, Westerners who pigeonholed Chinese facts into Western conceptions misconstrued China as a nation with a single centralized government in full operation. Dewey argued that China was not a nation, but at best, a nation-to-be. In his view, China was more like older Europe than contemporary France. Patriotism, Dewey observed, took a special form in China. It was not allegiance to a political state but an attachment to soil and birthplace. The Western conception of the nation-state could not be universalized across cultures. Moreover, Western economic terms do not fit the Chinese context. He said, "When we turn from political to economic affairs, our habitual western ideas are even less applicable. Their irrelevancy makes it impossible intelligently to describe the Chinese conditions or even grasp them intelligently." The most salient fact was that "there is no bourgeoisie in China." Dewey asked, "How is a class of peasant proprietors who form not merely the vast mass of a people but its economic and moral backbone, who traditionally and in present esteem [constitute] the respectable part of the population, next to the scholars, to be classified under western notions?" (MW 13: 75). Dewey insisted that China was politically and economically a different world and should be understood and treated as such.

Not only is China a politically and economically different world, but it is socially different as well. An example of Dewey's penetrating insights into Chinese social psychology is his analysis of Chinese people's "crowd psychology" that contributed to their conservatism and passivity. As Dewey observed in "What Holds China Back?":

> It is beyond question that many traits of the Chinese mind are the products of an extraordinary and long-continued density of populations. Psychologists have discovered, or possibly invented, a "psychology of the crowd" to account for the way men act in masses, as a mob at a lynching bee. They have not inquired as to the effect upon the mind of constant living in close contact with large numbers, of continual living in a crowd. Years ago an enthusiastic American teacher of the Chinese in Honolulu told me that when the Chinese acquired Anglo-Saxon initiative they would be the greatest people in the world. I wonder whether even the Anglo-Saxons would have developed or retained initiative if they had lived for centuries under conditions that gave them no room to stir about, no relief from the unremitting surveillance of their fellows? Possibly they would then have acquired a habit of thinking of their "face" before they thought of the thing to be done. Perhaps when they thought of a new thing they would have decided discretion and hesitation to be the better part of invention. If solitude or loneliness exists in China it is only among the monks who have retired into the mountain fastnesses; and until I have ocular evidence to the contrary I shall believe that even monks in China are sociable, agglutinative beings. (MW 12: 53)

Dewey's sympathetic rendering of the Chinese "face-loving" habit is unprecedented. He said, "When people live close together and cannot get away from one another, appearances, that is to say the impression made upon others, become as important as the realities, if not more so" (MW 12: 58). As he continued, "Until the recent introduction of rapid transportation, very few Chinese ever enjoyed even the possibility of solitude that comes from being in a crowd of strangers." "Imagine all elbow-room done away with, imagine millions of men living day by day, year by year, in the presence of the same persons (a very close presence at that), and new light may be shed upon the conservatism of the Chinese people." Dewey also told his U.S. readers, "Live and let live is the response to crowded conditions," and "Not to rock the boat is wisdom the world over" (MW 12: 55). If things are going well, then trying to make them better is pointless. If things are worse, enduring them is easier than seeking solutions and risking making things worse.

Dewey described vividly how such mental habits were played out in the process of attempts at reform. He wrote:

The reformer does not even meet sharp, clear-cut resistance. If he did, he might be stimulated to further effort. He simply is smothered. Stalling has become a fine art. At a recent national educational conference a returned student holding an official position moved that the public middle schools (corresponding to our high schools) be made co-educational. He was inspired by sound consideration. China suffers from [a] lack of educated women. Funds are short. The effective thing is to admit girls to the schools already existing. But the proposition was a radical innovation. Yet it was not opposed. A resolution in favor was duly passed. But at the same time it was made subtly understood that this was done out of courtesy to the mover, and that no steps to carry the resolution into effect need be expected. This is the fate of many proposed social reforms. They are not fought, they are only swallowed. China does not stagnate, it absorbs. It takes up all the slack till there is no rope left with which to pull. (MW 12: 55)

This was the frustrating reality of many reforms in China. Dewey's deepened understanding of the Chinese social and political psychology is the result of a long, searching process filled with high moments as well as low ones.

In one article, Dewey analyzed the three mental stages that a visitor in China was most likely to experience. The first stage was characterized by "impatience with irregularities, incompetence and corruptions, and a demand for immediate sweeping reforms" (MW 12: 48). Dewey's disappointment was evident when he wrote, "As with the drama of the Chinese stage, the main story is apparently lost in a mass of changing incidents and excitements that lack movement, climax and plot" (MW 11: 204). When he found that many students returning from the United States could not find better jobs other than teaching English, he asked, "How they can tolerate such corrupt, cruel and inefficient officials and govt, and have themselves so much intelligence, skill and real administrative power I give up [sic]. Militarism is bad enough but a pacifist militarism beats anything the world has seen. Non [resistants] ought to take a trip to China to be cured."[20]

The second stage is characterized by an understanding that China's enduring history and long-standing tradition had shaped its current conditions. Dewey commented, "The foreign interpreter comes to the scene with a mind adapted to the quick tempo of the West. He expects to see a drama unfold after the pattern of the movie. He is not used to history enacted on the scale of that of China" (MW 11: 205). Dewey elaborated, "Longer stay convinces him of the deep roots of many of the objectionable things, and gives him a new lesson in the meaning of the words 'evolution' and 'development'" (MW 12: 48). However, according to Dewey, many foreigners who had stayed in China for a long time remained complacent in this stage and did not support any attempts to modernize the country. Disheartened by current social chaos, these foreigners clung to the good old days allegiance to tradition guaranteed. They opposed all reforms, including the spread of popular education and the emancipation of women. In the third stage, the visitor "emerges where he no longer expects immediate sweeping changes, nor carps at the evils of the present in comparison with an idealized picture of the traditional past," but "feels that while now the endeavors for a new life are scattered, yet they are so numerous and so genuine that in time they will accumulate and coalesce" (MW 12: 49).

Throughout his stay, Dewey oscillated between hope and frustration. "History may be ransacked to furnish a situation that so stirs interest, that keeps a spectator so wavering between hope and fear, that presents so baffling a face to every attempt to find a solution" (MW 13: 95). In his low moments, he felt, "China remains a massive blank and impenetrable wall," and "Chinese civilization is so thick and [self-centered] that no foreign influence presented via a foreigner even scratches the surface."[21] At one point, Dewey felt so pessimistic about the situation that he revealed to his close friend Albert Barnes, "The western world is rotten, but it is distinctively in advance of China."[22] However, when Barnes asked whether Dewey really meant what he said, Dewey did not pursue this subject further.[23] Apparently, the comment is an expression of frustration, not a seriously considered judgment.

At other moments, Dewey felt that he had a better understanding of China's problems. He noted that China's political chaos was "the result of pure ignorance." As he explained, "One realizes how the delicate and multifarious business of the modern state is dependent upon knowledge and habits of mind that have grown up slowly and that are now counted upon as a matter of course" (MW 12: 49). Toward the end of his stay, Dewey said that he would like to stay another year "to see what happens," but he knew that "there would still be the waiting to see something definite happen."[24] In spite of all the difficulties, obscurities, and uncertainties, Dewey remained concerned and sympathetic. He continued to write about China for years after his departure. One article Dewey wrote after he returned to the United States deserves special attention because it contains the conclusions about his inquiry and his education in China. Dewey may not have been a great prophet in a world that was constantly changing, a world that operated under habits of mind often contrary to his own. His perseverance in learning led him to the ultimate understanding that China was not only a politically, economically, and socially different world, but also, more important, a philosophically different world, a world that could be understood only in its own philosophical terms.

The article under discussion, "As the Chinese Think," was first published in *Asia* in January 1922 and later republished in *Characters and Events* in 1929 with the title, "The Chinese Philosophy of Life." Dewey began by stating that people in different regions of the world "have different philosophies ingrained in their habits," and "an attempt at an honest understanding of one another's philosophy of life" was crucial to eliminating international disputes that often resulted from deep-seated misunderstandings. He then repeated the many questions that constantly baffled him during his stay in China. Dewey asked, "Why are the Chinese so unperturbed by circumstances that appear to a foreigner to menace their country with national extinction? . . . Is their attitude one of callous indifference, of stupid ignorance? Or is it a sign of faith in deep-seated realities that western peoples neglect in their hurry to get results?" He wondered, "Why hasn't China taken the lead in developing her own resources? . . . Is her course stupid inertia, a dull, obstinate clinging to the old just because it is old? Or does it show something more profound, a wise, even if largely unconscious, aversion to admitting forces that are hostile to the whole spirit of her civilization?" After a long and deep grappling with these questions, Dewey considered the possible explanation that "industrialism as it exists in the western world is a menace to what is deepest and best in Chinese culture," adding, "Only those who are completely satisfied with the workings of the present capitalistic system can dogmatically deny this possibility" (MW 13: 220–21).

After Dewey pointed out the hypothesis regarding the inherent conflict between indigenous Chinese beliefs and Western industrial practices, he turned to an analysis of Daoism's impact on the conservatism of Chinese people. Dewey specifically referred to Laozi's teachings: the doctrine of the superiority of nature to man and the concept of *wuwei*, often translated as nondoing. Dewey here rendered these notions in a way few Westerners could surpass in sympathy and penetration. As he contended:

> [The idea of nondoing] is nothing more than mere inactivity; it is a kind of rule of moral doing, a doctrine of active patience, endurance, persistence while nature has time to do her work. Conquering by yielding is its motto. The workings of nature will in time bring to naught the artificial fussings and fumings of man. Give enough rope to the haughty and ambitious, and in the end they will surely be hung in the artificial entanglements they have themselves evolved. (MW 13: 222)

Dewey stated that Laozi's teachings were influential in China because they had long been integrated into her agrarian habits of life. In his reading about Chinese agriculture, Dewey learned that "while western peoples have attacked, exploited and in the end wasted the soil, [the Chinese] have conserved it." He believed "this unparalleled human achievement in agriculture" accounted much for the conservatism of the Chinese because they had "learned to wait for the fruition of slow natural processes" and "because in their mode of life nature cannot be hustled" (MW 13: 222–23).

Dewey found the major key to the answers he had been searching for. He reminded his U.S. readers that the way the Chinese dealt with their political and social problems would always remain unintelligible unless their philosophy of life was taken into account. Dewey insisted, "To achieve anything worth while [*sic*] in our relations with the Chinese we have to adopt enough of their own point of view to recognize the importance of time. We must give them time and then more time; we must take time ourselves while we give them time" (MW 13: 223). Nonetheless, Dewey was not uncritical of the downsides of such lassiez-faire reverence for nature. He said, "Non-doing runs easily into passive submission, conservatism into stubborn attachment to habitudes so fixed as to be 'natural,' into dread and dislike of change." He held "the Chinese philosophy of life embodies a profoundly valuable contribution to human culture and one of which a hurried, impatient, over-busied and anxious West is indefinitely in need" (MW 13: 223).

Interestingly, the English philosopher Bertrand Russell shared and popularized this view in his *The Problem of China* (1922)—the result of his nine-month stay in China. It is highly likely that Russell's book came out after Dewey's "As the Chinese Think" and that Russell might even have read this article, although no definitive evidence exists. Because Russell's book was filled with exaltations of Chinese culture and civilization, the Republican president Dr. Sun Yat-sen praised the British philosopher as one of the few Westerners who truly understood China.[25] Unfortunately, the president did not mention the U.S. philosopher. If Dr. Sun had known that Russell at one point thought that the Beijing government of China was so corrupt that "fifty years of foreign domination is the only hope," Sun would probably have reconsidered his view of Russell.[26]

It is interesting to speculate why Dewey did not write a book on China as did Bertrand Russell, who once wrote that "I don't think that I shall write on China—it is a complex country, with an old civilization, very hard to fathom."[27] While Dewey was in China, a publisher wrote to him, expressing great eagerness to publish a volume of his essays on China.[28] Walter Lippmann also wrote to Dewey, encouraging him to write a special book on China and assuring him that more than one publisher had already expressed interest.[29] A simple and obvious reason why Dewey declined the opportunity might be that he had said all he needed to say about China in dozens of his articles and thus did not want to repeat himself. On closer examination, Dewey's decision was, in fact, quite consistent with his commitment to interpret China on its own terms. Knowing that China was going through a series of rapid changes and that the terms employed to interpret China at one time might seem superfluous or irrelevant at others, Dewey was modest and wise enough not to assume the role of expert or prophet. In his review of Russell's book, Dewey indicated that Russell's treatment of China in a straightforward and clear-cut manner overlooked underlying obscurities and ambiguities. As Dewey put it, Russell made "a lucid exposition of the external, or political and economic, problem of China—with a lucidity which, emerging from an obscure world, must always be close, as it is with Mr. Russell, to irony" (MW 15: 217). Dewey further remarked, "probably no one but a Chinese can give it to the world, a picture of the most wonderful as well as the most difficult to bring to conclusion of any that human history has yet witnessed" (MW 15: 18).

Furthermore, Dewey's decision not to write a book on China might also reflect an unwillingness to use the portrait of China—with its contrasting images and ideas—to define Europe. As Dewey said in his review of Russell's book, Russell portrayed China as "an angel of light to show up the darkness of western civilization," but failed to touch on the problem of China's internal transformation. Dewey concluded, "As a good European, he [Russell] is perhaps chiefly interested in European culture and what Europe has to learn from Asia; in comparison the stupendous and marvelous problem of the intrinsic remaking of the oldest, thickest, and most extensive civilization of the world does not attract his attention" (MW 15: 218). Unlike Russell who constructed an elevated image of Chinese virtues as a weapon to lash out against the vices of Western industrialism and imperialism, Dewey viewed China neither retrospectively nor instrumentally, but prospectively.[30] In his look toward the future of China, Dewey was willing to remain a sympathetic observer and an eloquent defender, rather than an authoritative expert.

Most important, Dewey's attitude toward China was a liberal one, as Remer observed in 1920: "[Dewey's] thought [about China] is not of the apologetic sort; it is experimental. This makes him a liberal thinker in the true sense; there is an air of freedom and hope about him. He does not, as many do, pay lip service to liberalism while his mind is set upon the main chance and 'safety first.'" Remer continued, "[Dewey] has helped the people of the United States to get a fair and honest appreciation of the activities of the Chinese" and should be honored as a "true servant of his country and of the people of his time."[31] Even though nothing was improper about Remer's patriotic glorification of Dewey, I think Dewey's concern for China came from "his intellectual interest [as] an observer of the affairs of humanity," as he himself put it (MW 13:75). His concern for China persisted in the remainder of his life. At age eighty-six, Dewey even planned to visit China for the second time.[32] China was indeed the country "nearest to his heart after his own" as his daughter remarked.[33]

In his book *To Change China: Western Advisors in China, 1620–1960* (1980), Jonathan Spence studies sixteen Westerners who were advisors in China. He does not include Dewey, who proved to be a good contrast to these advisors. According to Spence, they assumed an air of superiority, believing that their goal to "make China more like the West" was morally legitimate. In a way, they expected the Chinese to accept their expertise along with their ideologies. Because the Chinese viewed accepting a foreign ideology on foreign terms as a form of submission, they eventually resisted. The repercussions of this conflict left these Western advisors feeling betrayed and despondent about "the loss of China." If Spence's study of the Western advisors in China speaks to us about "the indefinable realm where altruism and exploitation meet," my study of Dewey assures us that intellectual humility and open-mindedness can prevent the dangers of uninformed altruism.[34] Dewey recalled years later that he arrived in China "in a state of blissful ignorance, with no operation of culture weighing me down," but he returned with a deepened understanding of human societies and cultures.[35] Realizing that genuine social change was slow in coming, Dewey acknowledged that China would eventually stand on its own.

Dewey came to China at the perfect time for his own learning. His teaching, however, was compromised by the intellectual climate during the May Fourth era. Owing to the ideological divisiveness of the time, Chinese intellectuals tended to use Dewey to serve their own agendas rather than to engage his ideas directly. They either hailed him as a savior or denigrated him as a false god. In fact, one senses that Dewey's status as a teacher was symbolic at best. His teachings were largely mediated through the interpretations of Hu Shih, who differed from Dewey in many important ways. Hu advocated wholesale assimilation to Western values and beliefs, whereas Dewey hoped that China would maintain the strengths in her own culture as a basis for future development. Dewey understood that democracy for China had to come from her own cultural roots rather than from the imposition by foreign influences. Unfortunately, Chinese intellectuals, including his own disciple Hu, failed to take his advice. In the end, the biggest beneficiary of this intercultural exchange was perhaps Dewey himself.

A Fruitful Journey to the East

In many ways, Dewey's visit to China was like an adventure to him. In the beginning, he did not know what to expect; in the end, he realized that he could not have asked for a more interesting and fruitful journey than the one he had in China. Now I would like to discuss the other meanings of Dewey's journey in the larger context of his life and work—a timely rest, a spiritual harbor, a professional opportunity, an international recognition, and an intellectual rejuvenation.

Apart from the educational value of Dewey's visit to China, the trip itself was a significant and rewarding experience in many other aspects. First and foremost, it offered a good rest that Dewey truly needed at the time. During the years prior to his departure, Dewey had engrossed himself in political commentary and struggled to bring his pragmatic ideas to bear on World War I politics. The struggle turned out to be not only intellectually draining, but also emotionally disturbing. Dewey's support for U.S. intervention in the war led to a heated dispute with his pacifist friends, Ralph Bourne and Jane Addams. In particular, Dewey's endorsement of the war as an intelligent use of force generated a bitter confrontation with Bourne, who accused Dewey of betraying his own democratic principles. As Steven Rockefeller pointed out, "After years of hard work and strife on the forefront of social reform, Dewey was exhausted emotionally and physically. His poems are filled with expressions of a craving for rest, sunlit gardens, or a time to enjoy 'sweet soft things alluring,' and on occasion he discloses a desire for the peace and forgetfulness of death."[36] Perceived in this light, Dewey's long sojourn in the Far East was important in the sense that it enabled him to recover from psychological fatigue and to heal emotional wounds.

As Dewey pondered over whether he should stay in China for the second year, he wrote to a colleague at Columbia University, saying that staying "seemed the easiest thing to do, especially as reports from America aren't especially attractive so far as living is concerned." Dewey also emphasized that he wanted to "clinch whatever may have got started" in the first year.[37] Later, he admitted to another friend that "life here is very easy and comfortable and neither Mrs. Dewey nor myself is anxious to undergo the stress of home conditions. China is a paradise for old people who don't want responsibility."[38] In one sense, China was a safe haven where Dewey could temporarily detach himself from all the political hassles at home. Although his presence in China opened his eyes to the dark realities of international politics, it also sheltered him from criticisms for his idealistic support for the war. The defeat of idealist aims at the Versailles Peace Conference could have been a harder blow on Dewey had he not been abroad. Dewey was able to walk out of the traumatic shadows of war politics so that he could return home physically rested and mentally refreshed. Immediately after he returned, Dewey took up a leading position in the Outlawry of War movement that urged an international law against initiating warfare.

Dewey's trip to the Far East also marked a turning point in his life as a public intellectual. The articles he published in the *New Republic* and *Asia* provided him the opportunity to reclaim his reputation in intellectual circles. Judging from Walter Lippmann's praise of his articles, one can see that Dewey's role as a political commentator in China must have gained wide recognition. Moreover, Dewey's letters from Japan and China were so popular among family members that his daughter Jane Dewey compiled them into a book to share with the public.[39] The reviews of the book were generally positive. The Deweys were praised for their "simplicity of manner and willingness to absorb local atmosphere and customs"; for their nonpropagandist viewpoint and human touch, which were "quite impossible [to find] in a work constructed to prove a case or a theory"; and for their natural depictions, which "make you feel that you have seen China quite as truly as if you had been there."[40] The popularity and recognition Dewey enjoyed because of his affiliation with China are apparent. Dewey's colleagues at Columbia University even expected him to teach a course based on his experiences in the Far East when he returned.[41]

Furthermore, the fruitful experiences Dewey gained from his extensive travel in Asia made him all the more convinced of the interconnectedness between nations in the world. After his trip, Dewey felt more certain about the importance of understanding other cultures and of bridging territorial, national boundaries. As Jay Martin says, after his trips to Japan and China, Dewey "had become a changed person, more precisely, an evolving person. His educational vision and his political understanding had broadened beyond American boundaries to include the world."[42] Dewey was indeed transformed by his trip to the Far East from U.S. philosopher to a transnational philosopher. In addition, after his visit to China, Dewey maintained his noninterventionist approach to international politics, as evidenced in his attitude toward Nicaragua and Mexico.[43]

Dewey's visit to China and his efforts to help modernize China's schools, which were widely reported and recognized, led to many invitations from other foreign governments to inspect their education systems. His subsequent educational missions—Turkey in 1924, Mexico in 1926, Russia in 1928, and South Africa in 1934—are the result of this international reputation. In addition, the experiences and education Dewey had in China allowed him to adapt quickly to foreign places and produce insightful work in a short period of time. As one Turkish scholar said admiringly, "Written with a broad view, sympathetic and analytic, both demanding and understanding, Dewey's report [on Turkey's educational system] is a model of its genre."[44]

Moreover, Dewey's visit marked an intellectual rejuvenation. He wrote to a colleague, "Nothing western looks quite the same an[y] more, and this is as near to a renewal of youth as can be hoped for in this world."[45] Moreover, Dewey's international trips helped shaped his later philosophical writing, such as *The Quest for Certainty* (1929). As Jay Martin writes:

> Much of his earlier philosophical work was present in [*The Quest for Certainty*] but tempered by the political lessons he had learned in China, Turkey, Mexico, and most recently, the Soviet Union. In each he believed he had seen the stirrings of a modern revolution against established institutions and beliefs. He did not have to look back to medieval Europe to see what he was describing; he had seen in person the conflict between the quest for certainty and the wish for security, counterpoised to the pressure of change.[46]

The visit to China can be seen as demarcating a watershed in Dewey's general intellectual development. In preparing for his numerous lectures in China on topics ranging from education, ethics, and pragmatism to political theories and Greek philosophy, Dewey had exhausted much of what he knew and had thought out. After repeating these ideas again and again in these lectures, Dewey must have been eager to refresh his mind when he returned. Even though he did not do any philosophical reading while he was in China, he was actively practicing philosophy in the form of cultural and political criticism. This "two-year hiatus" actually pushed his philosophical thinking and encouraged him to "begin anew."[47] The next chapter looks at the way Dewey rendered his social and political ideas "anew" as a result of the two-year trip.

CHAPTER 5

THE INFLUENCE OF CHINA ON DEWEY'S SOCIAL AND POLITICAL PHILOSOPHY

❖

The previous chapter explored Dewey's learning experiences in China during his visit. This chapter is devoted to tracing Dewey's intellectual development in relation to his visit to China, focusing mainly on his social and political philosophy. I compare Dewey's political writings during the twelve years between *German Philosophy and Politics* (1915) and *The Public and Its Problems* (1927). To expound the thesis of Dewey's intellectual development, I also draw on his earlier and later writings wherever relevant and appropriate. Importantly, we should note that Dewey's thinking was always evolving. The arguments I make concerning the development of Dewey's ideas do not exclude other factors in his life and thinking that may have contributed to the development. In addition, I understand that I am presenting only plausible but not conclusive arguments concerning how China may have influenced Dewey. Despite these caveats, his visit to China undoubtedly stimulated his thinking, and the contours of his philosophy were expanded as a result. Having an alternative place to stand and from which to look, Dewey was able to review his ideas in a fresh light. Above all, when Dewey's philosophy and his experiences in China are considered together, we get a fuller understanding of his ideas.

Rethinking Internationalism

Dewey's support for U.S. participation in World War I reflected a rejection of isolationism and an affirmation of internationalism. Unlike those who thought that the United States could remain isolated and thus protected from the political crises that were plaguing Europe, Dewey understood that the destiny of any one nation in the modern epoch was invariably linked to the rest of the world and that isolationism was not only undesirable but also impossible. Nonetheless, embracing internationalism was one thing, but knowing what it entailed was quite another. How, for example, would the colonial world order be replaced by a democratic one? What would this new democratic order look like? Or was the attempt to "make the world safe for democracy" simply a high-sounding slogan? Are wars between nations inevitable?

In his earlier writings, Dewey was primarily concerned with the political implications of internationalism. He saw an urgent need to establish a political agency or machinery that would mediate disputes and facilitate communication among nations. Much to the dismay of his pacifist friends, Dewey considered the war a means for realizing the possibility of "a democratically ordered international government" and "the subsequent beginning of the end of war" (MW 11: 181). He thought that genuine love of peace obligated one to establish "the machinery, the specific, concrete social arrangements . . . for maintaining peace" (MW 10: 263). Peace in and of itself was only a negative idea. "There were ideals more important than keeping one's body whole and one's property intact" (MW 8: 203). During the war years, Dewey believed that future human prosperity and peace depended on new international agencies of cooperation and control, the establishment of which, he thought, would foreclose the nineteenth-century idea of independent, isolated nation-states, thereby ushering in a new century of internationalism.

The new age of internationalism also required a reexamination of existing political theories, which had dealt largely with internal questions about the relationships between the individual and society. This internal focus tended to leave untouched important questions about the proper relations between nations. The war in Europe represented the failure to acknowledge and deal with the wider, cross-cultural relationships created through free trade and assisted by modern methods of transportation and communication. It signified a breakdown in the relations between independent nations. Dewey said, "In commerce, we are proceeding on an international basis," but in politics, "we are doing business . . . upon the basis of isolated international sovereignty." We must "either internationalize our antiquated political machinery or we must make our commercial ideas and practices conform to our political"(MW 10: 241–42).

The onset of war in Europe propelled Dewey to inquire into the nature and problems of the nation-state. Dewey sought to reexamine the political tradition of the West to diagnose causes for contemporary international problems. He took as his point of departure one of the defining moments of modern Western civilization, namely, the rise of the individual. As Dewey observed, the individual emerged in the modern West as the center of legal rights and responsibilities. Attendant on this emergence was that of the territorial nation-state as an enlarged individual possessing its own identity, authority, and sovereignty. For Dewey, the conception of sovereignty as the essence of the state proved to be most pernicious. As sovereignty stipulated absolute authority within the state and complete independence from without, it literally maintained a perpetual condition of international anarchy. As Donald Koch notes, Dewey was convinced that "the moral ideas connected with the sovereign state and later the national state are inadequate to deal with the current international situation" and that new ways of construing international relations needed to be created.[1]

At this time, the major target of Dewey's internationalism was the idea of national sovereignty. In his *German Philosophy and Politics*, Dewey set out to attack this obsolete European idea and to replace it with the new American ideal of international democracy. Even though the book was sometimes denigrated as a call to war, it was actually intended, Gary Bullert argues, to assist the United States in the process of establishing its own political theories and ideals.[2] As Dewey pleaded, "We must make the accident of our internal composition into an idea, an idea upon which we may conduct our foreign as well as our domestic policy. An international judicial tribunal will break in the end upon the principle of national sovereignty" (MW 8: 203). Dewey urged Americans to forsake the idea of national sovereignty, reminding them that their history was different from that of Europe. Interracial and international in composition, the United States was uniquely suited to develop the ideal of internationalism. He said that unless Americans were willing to forgo national sovereignty and submit their domestic and foreign policies to an international legislature, they had no legitimate reasons to criticize other warring nations.

Throughout the war years and before his departure to the Far East, the idea of an international, democratic government dominated Dewey's thinking about internationalism, which can be rightly characterized as politically rather than culturally oriented. Through April 1919 before the setbacks of democratic ideals at the Versailles Peace Conference became a reality, Dewey still pledged support for a vigorous League of Nations. Even though he said that democracy meant more than a government, his writings at the time implicitly assumed that international democracy began with a democratic international government. This view may have reflected the contingencies of wartime politics, rather than a clear and potent vision of international democracy. The content of the Versailles peace treaty exposed the inadequacy of this view and forced Dewey to reconsider the meaning of internationalism. Dewey attributed the defeat of American war ideals at the conference to "immaturity and inexperience in international politics" (MW 11: 182). Significantly, his visit to China came in time to provide him the very lesson he needed because China happened to be, as Dewey put it, "a great place to study international politics."[3] On arrival, he realized that the crisis in the Far East "is infinitely more serious than we realize at home."[4] Fearing that either Japan or Russia would occupy China, Dewey said that "a genuine League of Nations—one with some vigor—is the only salvation I can see of the whole Eastern situation." This may be an offhand remark, but it showed that when Dewey had just arrived in China, he still hoped that the League of Nations would enforce justice, even with the proviso—"if only by any chance there is a League—which looks most dubious at this distance."[5]

Half a year into his stay in China, Dewey's doubtful hope for a genuine League of Nations to serve as China's guardian was completely thwarted. As he reflected, there was simply no "sufficient amount of disinterested intelligence to perform such a task" (MW 11: 213). Dewey's wish that governments working together could bring about significant change did not realize because international politics was largely governed by secret diplomacy and fierce competition of economic interests, all pointing invariably to the duplicity of political rhetoric and the superficiality of political machinery. Referring to the failure at the Versailles Peace Conference, Dewey said, "If the United States in working with the Allies was obliged to surrender at Paris . . . China prefers to trust a United States which is free from such commitments and entanglements." He added that "a United States which was going it alone" would be more effective in realizing true internationalism than "a United States in a League the other members of which had no belief in American ideals" (MW 11: 198). The role of guardianship Dewey assigned to the United States at this point was largely moral and intellectual. As he reminded his U.S. readers, "We stay on safe ground if we confine ourselves to saying that to be successful such a guardian would have to confine his efforts to stimulating, encouraging and expediting the democratic forces acting from within" (MW 11: 213–14). However, Dewey later came to see that even such a role of well-intended guardianship was itself morally dubious.

Dewey's growing understanding of the limitations of political internationalism and the problems of cultural misunderstanding led him to the realization that "democracy in international relations is not a matter of agencies but of aims and consequences" (MW 11: 198). The ideal of international democracy should not be focused on establishing a "democratically ordered international government," "a World Federation," "International Tribunal," or "League of Nations," nor should it be focused on arranging "international" tutelage for so-called backward countries. Dewey expressed this realization mostly vividly in the article, "Our National Dilemma," in which he attempted to dissect U.S. national psychology. As he wrote, Americans had a genuine "preference for" and yet a "halting attachment" to "democracy in politics," to the ideals of "responsible government and publicity" (MW 12: 4). Dewey's exposure to Chinese habits of mind, which run counter to Western beliefs and practices, led to these reflections:

> To the student of political and social development, China presents a most exciting intellectual situation. He has read in books the account of the slow evolution of law and orderly governmental institutions. He finds in China an object lesson in what he has read. We take for granted the existence of government as an agency for enforcing justice between men and for protecting personal rights. We depend upon regular and orderly legal and judicial procedure to settle disputes as we take for granted the atmosphere we breathe. In China life goes on practically without such support and guarantees. And yet in the ordinary life of the people peace and order reign. (MW 12: 41)

Even though Dewey may have overstated the orderliness of the lives of ordinary people in China, the contrast he perceived was evident enough to suggest to him the fallibility of Western political habitudes, namely, the overreliance on government as an organ for social justice and world peace.

As a matter of fact, internationalism was better exemplified in the effort to guard one nation's own domestic policies against untoward consequences of events in other nations, rather than in the attempt to force other nations to comply with one's presumed universal rules and ideals, either in the name of a policeman or a guardian. In "Our Share in Drugging China," Dewey attempted to make this point. He began by saying, "Of the millions who associate opium and China probably only few know, beyond a vague impression of England's part in an 'Opium War,' that from the very beginning, the responsibility for introduction and spread of the use of narcotics lies with foreign nations" (MW 11: 235). He went on to explain how tons of parcels containing illegal drugs arrived in China through a process of "international cooperation." These products were shipped by the manufacturers in Scotland to the United States, reshipped from the United States to Japan, and finally smuggled from Japan to the coastal dealers in China. Dewey said that U.S. participation in the whole process of poisoning China lay in a policy that allowed the drugs to be vaguely labeled as "pharmaceutical products," insisting that "the primary responsibility is with the laws and administration of the United States" (MW 11: 239). He urged the U.S. government to frame laws and regulations that would compel adequate registration of all opium products reaching its ports and would make retransporting such products for export a crime. Dewey believed that this change of domestic policy in response to its international consequences was a surer way to secure internationalist ideals than a corrupt League of Nations or an international tutelage with a hidden imperialistic agenda.

In light of the inadequacy of political internationalism, Dewey shifted his emphasis to the cultural manifestations of internationalism. He wrote, "The atmosphere that makes international troubles inflammable is the product of deep-seated misunderstandings that have their origin in different philosophies of life" (MW 13: 218). The way to "fire-proof international relations," Dewey said, "must begin with an attempt at an honest understanding of one another's philosophy of life." As he elaborated:

> The common belief at the present time that the Pacific is to be the scene of the next great world catastrophe, the fatalistic belief that conflict between the white and the yellow race[s] is predestined, are really expressions of a sense of a deep, underlying cleft that makes cultural understanding impossible. But instead of trying to lesson [sic] the cleft by effort to understand each other, we talk about an irrepressible conflict of forces beyond human control, or else about the competition for control of the natural sources of China and the tropics. . . . If we succeed in really understanding each other, some way of cooperation for common ends can be found. If we neglect the part played by fundamental misunderstandings in developing an atmosphere of combustion, any devices that are hit upon for lessoning [sic] economic friction are likely to turn out so superficial that soon[er] or later they will break down. (MW 13: 218–19)

Democracy in international relations should be based not only on the establishment of political organizations, but also on the foundation of cultural understanding. The more we understand one another's cultures, the more we are likely to form an international community.

How, then, do we understand one another's cultures? To put into practice his newfound belief in the importance of cultural understanding, Dewey seized every opportunity he had to travel outside of the United States to continue his learning about different cultures and to sharpen his views about international politics. During the years between 1924 and 1934, Dewey visited Turkey, Mexico, Russia, and South Africa while diligently recording his observations and reporting them to his fellow Americans. However, cultural understanding neither begins nor ends with foreign trips. It is a mindset and an attitude fostered by local experience. Democracy, be it domestic or international, has its origin in "the neighborly community." As Dewey wrote in *The Public and Its Problems*:

> It is said, and said truly, that for the world's peace it is necessary that we understand the peoples of foreign lands. How well do we

understand, I wonder, our next door neighbors? It has also been said that if a man love not his fellow man whom he has seen, he cannot love the God whom he has not seen. The chances of regard for distant peoples being effective as long as there is no close neighborhood experience to bring with it insights and understanding of neighbors do not seem better. A man who has not been seen in the daily relations of life may inspire admiration, emulation, servile subjection, fanatical partisanship, hero worship; but not love and understanding, save as they radiate from the attachments of a near-by union. Democracy must begin at home, and its home is the neighborly community. (LW 2: 368)

Dewey believed that because the United States is intercultural and interracial in composition, the consolidation of local communities comprising people of different ethnicities and nationalities would lead to cultural understanding.

Dewey once cautioned, "it is ridiculous to suppose that the problems of the Pacific can be settled in a few weeks, or months—or years" (MW 13: 172). Likewise, democracy in international relations was not to be achieved in months, in years, or even in decades because it depends on enlightened communication based on a solid foundation of cultural understanding. There is no shortcut to cultural understanding; only frequent contacts, amicable interaction, open communication, and intelligent inquiry can gradually bring it about. Resort to military force or political authority is a step backward in this process. Victories in wars, however apparently legitimate and glorious, are always self-destructive because they breed within them the seeds of ever more hostility, ever more loss of human lives, and ever more denigration of human dignity. The wars may have been won, but the people definitely will have lost.

Replacing the State with the Public

Since the outbreak of World War I, Dewey had been reflecting on the problem concerning the idealization of the nation-state. In his *German Philosophy and Politics*, Dewey set out to reject Hegel's metaphysical formulation of the state as the embodiment of absolute spirit, as "God on earth," which lies beyond the criticism of reason and experience. Dewey thought that Hegel was writing the entire history of humanity in nationalistic terms. In Hegel's formulation, "The State is the Individual of history; it is to history what a given man is to biography. History gives us the progressive realization or evolution of the Absolute, moving from one National Individual to another. It is law, the universal, which makes the State a State" (MW 8: 195). Hegel "ignores all future possibility of a genuinely international federation to which isolated nationalism shall be subordinated" (MW 8: 196). In *Reconstruction in Philosophy*, Dewey continued accusing Hegel of "[telling] us about *the* state when we want to know about *some* state," and of implying that "what is said about *the* state applies to any state that we happen to wish to know about" (MW 12: 188). Dewey's thinking at this point can be summed up in his repudiation of Hegel's theory and his endorsement of an international federation that would render obsolete the idea of national sovereignty. However, the question of what the state is, if not "God on earth," was still to be addressed.

Dewey did not develop his own theory of the state to replace Hegel's until he published *The Public and Its Problems* in 1927. However, the issue concerning the nature and scope of the nation-state occupied his mind during the interim years, particularly as he observed the process of China's development into a modern nation-state. Dewey argued that China was not a nation in terms of how nations came to be understood in Europe. China was diversified as Europe rather than homogeneous as France. However, Dewey assured that China was soon to become a nation, even though no one knew how long it would take and what kind of nation it would become. In one sense, Dewey's visit to China seemed like a trip back in time: the China he saw was like Europe before it was divided into several independent nation-states. This unique opportunity provided an actual historical and empirical context for him to dissect the concept of the nation-state. For instance, in the midst of his analyses of China's situation, Dewey raised these questions about the past and future of the nation-state:

> When did nations begin to be, anyway? How long has France been a compact and homogeneous nation? Italy, Germany? What forces made them nations? And what is going to be the future of the national state outside of China? What is the future of internationalism? Our whole concept of a nation is of such recent origin that it is not surprising that it does not fit in any exact way into Chinese conditions. And possibly the days in which political nationality is most fully established are also the days of its beginning to decline. (MW 13: 73)

Dewey was evidently questioning the permanence of the state with his suggestion about its possible decline. He actually developed this idea in *The Public and Its Problems*, where he claimed, "a state is ever something to be scrutinized, investigated, searched for. Almost as soon as its form is stabilized, it needs to be re-made" (LW 2: 255).

Before we consider how his experiences in China might have influenced the development of his thought, we need to examine Dewey's theory of the state. The theory was by no means elaborate; it derived from his notion of the public, which was the focus of his thinking. Dewey opened the discussion of chapter one, "Search for the Public," by surveying various theories of the state in the history of Western political thought. The state has been viewed as an ideal of "associated and harmonized life," "an arbiter in the conflict of other social units," or as an "organized oppression" (LW 2: 238–39). Though divergent and conflicting, these views resulted from the same attempt to "look for state-forming forces" (LW 2: 242). Dewey claimed that political philosophers before him "have looked in the wrong place," that is, "in the field of agencies, in that of doers of deeds, or in some will or purpose of authorship" (LW 2: 247). Taking the form of the state as a given, they envisioned "the State" as possessing an ontological reality of its own, independent of the fact that the actual forms of the state differ in different epochs, locales, and cultures. Dewey suggested that we search for the public to find the state because "if we look in the wrong place for the public, we shall never locate the state" (LW 2: 259).

To discover the public, and hence the state, Dewey called for a consequentialist approach: that is, starting with the facts of human activity and considering their consequences. He took as his point of departure the fact that "human acts have consequences upon others, and that some of these consequences are perceived, and that their perception leads to subsequent effort to control action so as to secure some consequences and avoid others" (LW 2: 243). Dewey proceeded to make a distinction between direct consequences, which affect the persons directly engaged, and indirect consequences, which extend beyond those immediately concerned. He claimed, "those indirectly and seriously affected for good or for evil form a group distinctive enough to require recognition and a name. The name selected is The Public" (LW 2: 257). As for the state, Dewey said that "the only statement which can be made is a purely formal one: the state is the organization of the public effected through officials for the protection of the interests shared by its members." What Dewey presented is a generic account of the state as it is, as it ought to be, and as it may become. His account may appear too simplistic to those looking for a grand theory. However, its significance lies in the possibilities it opened for future experimentation with the forms of the state. As he added, "what the public may be, what the officials are, how adequately they perform their function, are things we have to go to history to discover" (LW 2: 256).

For Dewey, the role of the public is primary, whereas the function of the state is subordinate. "There is no state without a government, but also there is none without the public" (LW 2: 277). The state is "a distinctive and secondary form of association, having a specifiable work to do and specified organs of operation." Therefore, one should not "assign all the values which are generated and maintained by means of human associations to the work of states" (LW 2: 279). Dewey knew of no better way to apprehend the absurdity of such presuppositions than "to call to mind the influence upon community life of Socrates, Buddha, Jesus, Aristotle, Confucius, Homer, Vergil [sic], Dante, St. Thomas, Shakespeare, Copernicus, Galileo, Newton, Boyle, Locke, Rousseau and countless others, and then to ask ourselves if we conceive these men to be officers" (LW 2: 253). Indeed, it makes no sense to exaggerate the authority of the state by granting it mystical or supernatural sanction. Likewise, it makes no sense to translate "all social values into political value" (LW 2: 280). The state comes into existence as a result of the operation of habits formed through the naturally associative character of human action. The state is but one element of society, the representation of one social interest. Unfortunately, in theory, it often takes precedence over all others.

In Dewey's view, both the public and the state have no fixed forms, the reasons being that different "conditions make the consequences of associated action and the knowledge of them different" and that "the means by which a public can determine the government to serve its interests vary" (LW 2: 256). The public can be local, national, or transnational, depending on the scope and quantity of extensive, enduring, serious consequences perceived and acknowledged as needing regulation. Dewey's pragmatic sensibility allowed him to break from existing political forms and to envision a new public generated in the modern era of human relationships. He urged that "non-political forces organize themselves to transform existing political structures: that the divided and troubled publics integrate" (LW 2: 315).

Nevertheless, Dewey understood the difficulty of this task because "the change of the forms of state is so often effected only by revolution." He lamented, "The creation of adequately flexible and responsive political and legal machinery has so far been beyond the wit of man" (LW 2: 255). As he said, "the treaty of Versailles is there to show how difficult it is to make a shift of personnel even when conditions radically alter so that there is need for men of a changed outlook and interests" (LW 2: 284–85). Even though changing existing political forms is difficult, that is what he proposed—only gradually, continuously, and experimentally. Because the conditions of human action and of social inquiry are always changing, "the experiment," as Dewey noted, "must always be retried; the State must always be rediscovered" (LW 2: 256). He further pointed out that political philosophy and science should not engage in determining "what the state in general should or must be," but "to aid in creation of methods such that experimentation may go on less blindly, less at the mercy of accident, more intelligently." Dewey reminded his U.S. readers: "The belief in political fixity, of the sanctity of some form of state consecrated by the efforts of our fathers and hallowed by tradition, is one of the stumbling-blocks in the way of orderly and directed change; it is an invitation to revolt and revolution" (LW 2: 256–57).

To answer the question of what may have contributed to the development of Dewey's thinking, many will immediately think of Walter Lippmann's *The Phantom Public* (1925), which provoked Dewey to write a defense of democracy, *The Public and Its Problems,* against Lippmann's charges. Although this may have been the immediate stimulus, it does not explain the content of Dewey's response. To understand that content, we need to link Dewey's political experiences in World War I and his subsequent experiences in China. First, the war had a huge impact on Dewey. In his support for U.S. participation in the war, Dewey relied on political institutions to implement change only to realize that he should not have taken political leaders' professed ideals for granted. At that time, Dewey lacked an understanding that "the type of man brought forward by war is not the type needed to make peace" (MW 11: 182). Figuratively speaking, Dewey had a brief romance with the state. Like most unsuccessful relationships, it ended in profound distrust—in this case, distrust of state institutions and government agencies as effective means of social change. Dewey's distrust of the state led him to remark years later that "one of the most regular activities of the politically organized community has been waging war" (LW 2: 245) and that "the world has suffered more from leaders and authorities than from the masses" (LW 2: 365). In fact, some scholars interpreted Dewey's political theories that advocate government without domination as "more anarchist" than "liberal."[6]

The impact of the war on Dewey fermented during his visit to the Far East. Overwhelmed by wartime politics, the fatigued Dewey traveled to Japan soon after the war ended. When the news of the Versailles Peace Conference broke, Dewey was arriving in China just in time to watch the prelude of a fascinating historical drama, namely, the May Fourth movement. As noted, Dewey was captivated by the power of public opinion manifested in the strikes of students and the boycotts of merchants. The image of a powerful public—independent of the state but in the end capable of controlling it—was deeply impressed on Dewey's mind. The events in China convinced him that political purposes could be effectively achieved through "moral and intellectual" force, as opposed to regular government channels and military means. Dewey said, "Even if nothing more were to come of the movement, it would be worth observation and record as an exhibition of the way in which China is really governed—when it is governed at all." He added:

American children are taught the list of "modern" inventions that originated in China. They are not taught, however, that China invented the boycott, the general strike and guild organization as means of controlling public affairs. In no other civilized country of the present day is brute force such a factor in official government as in China. But in no other country could moral and intellectual force accomplish so quickly and peaceably what was effected in China in the last five or six weeks. (MW 11: 191)

The tone of Dewey's writing seemed to convey his amazement and excitement.

Dewey was fascinated by the contrast he saw between an organized, integrated public and an incompetent, untrustworthy state. This experience helped turn his attention away from the state to the public. Nonetheless, I do not mean to suggest that Dewey thought that the state could be completely discarded or that he came to hold an "antipolitical bias" as his disciple Hu Shih did. As mentioned earlier, Dewey had doubted the efficacy of cultural reform alone in effecting social change. In his distrust of the state, Dewey did not become antipolitical. He simply took a different approach to politics: he realized that political action could be accomplished through the public rather than the state. The first two chapters of *The Public and Its Problems* can be construed as a deliberate attempt to clarify the point that the consolidation of the public is more important than that of the state.

Let me elaborate on the arguments just outlined and give more examples of how Dewey's exposure to Chinese political psychology and social reality reinforced his earlier denunciation of the supremacy of the state. In "Chinese National Sentiment," Dewey wrote:

The central factor in the Chinese historic political psychology is its profound indifference to everything that we associate with the state, with government. One inclines to wonder sometimes why the anarchists of the pacifist and philosophic type have not seized upon China as a working exemplification of their theories. Probably the reason is that being preoccupied with the problem of active abolition of government, they have not been able to conceive of an anarchy which should be only a profound apathy towards government. Or else they, too, have been misled by the popular association of anarchy with extreme freedom and mobility, and could not imagine it in connection with the stagnation attributed to China. (MW 11: 216)

The fact that China could sustain itself in the long course of human history with the majority of its people being indifferent to political questions was an eye-opener to Dewey. Even though China had been ruled by imperial governments, and sometimes despotic ones, the masses still went about their business of tilling and eating, begetting and dying. As Dewey described:

Governors come and go, and fuss about their petty intrigues of glory and greed. But they do not govern the farmers, who are the mass of the population. The only governance known to them is that of nature, the rules of the immemorial change of seasons, the fateful laws of birth and death, of seed-corn and harvest, of flood and pestilence. In the words of perhaps their oftenest quoted proverb, "Heaven is high and the Emperor far away." The implication is that earth is close and intimate, the family and village nearby. (MW 11: 217)

The central government of China, except on a few important ritual occasions, had nothing much to do with the ordinary lives of the people.

The West has embarked on a very different path because it "approaches all political questions with ideas composed on the pattern of a national state, with its sovereignty and definite organs, political, judicial, executive and administrative, to perform specific functions." As Dewey observed:

We have taken European political development as a necessary standard of normal political evolution. We have made ourselves believe that all development from savagery to civilization must follow a like course and pass through similar stages. When we find societies that do not agree with this standard we blandly dismiss them as abnormalities, as survivals of backward states, or as manifestations of lack of political capacity. (MW 11: 215).

Chinese institutions and ideas were considered malfunctioning or backward according to Western standards. "In actual fact," Dewey said, "they mark an extraordinary development in a particular direction," one that seems so strange and unfamiliar that "we dispose of them as a mass of hopeless political confusion and corruption." Dewey further praised this development as embodying "a high code of ethics without the blessings of a divine revelation" (MW 11: 215). The "particular direction" of development Dewey mentioned here resonated with what he later distinguished as social and moral democracy. I return to this point later in this chapter when I discuss the influence of China on his thinking about democracy.

Dewey saw nothing particularly sacred or universal in the political pattern of the West. Informed by the history of China's political development, he attempted to reconstruct Western political philosophy to reflect empirical facts and enhance experimental possibilities. Before Dewey went to China, he had only Western examples to draw on, which are limited as well as limiting. His analyses of Chinese history and politics enabled him to think outside of the Western box and to broaden his perspective. To counter universal claims about the state, Dewey used examples in Eastern cultures to support his central contention about the nature of the state, namely, its "temporal and local diversification." As he explained in *The Public and Its Problems*, "For long periods of human history, especially in the Orient, the state is hardly more than a shadow thrown upon the family and neighborhood by remote personages, swollen to gigantic form by religious beliefs. It rules but it does not regulate; for its rule is confined to receipt of tribute and ceremonial deference. Duties are within the family; property is possessed by the family" (LW 2: 261–62).

Dewey was impressed with Chinese politics because it "is not a branch of morals" but "submerged in morals" and because the value of the state "lies in what it does not do." A perfect state was regarded as being one with "the processes of nature, in virtue of which the seasons travel their constant round, so that fields under the beneficent rule of sun and rain produce their harvest, and the neighborhood prospers in peace" (LW 2: 262). The picture of Chinese political life, as Dewey understood it, may lie behind his claim that under some conditions, the state is "the most idle and empty of all social arrangements" (LW 2: 253). The evidence from the Chinese political history allowed Dewey to reject the presupposition of the state "as an archetypal entity" pervasive in Western political philosophy and science (LW 2: 264).

Dewey also pointed out some prejudices in the way Western nations positioned themselves in their contact with non-Western countries. As he wrote, "The idea that there is a model pattern which makes a state a good or true state . . . is responsible for the effort to form constitutions offhand and impose them ready-made on peoples" (LW 2: 264). Even though Dewey did not indicate which particular instance he was referring to, he might have been thinking of the case in China. For example, in his reports on contemporary Chinese events, Dewey depicted the newly established Republican government as a total disaster because it was imposed rather than developed from within. As he put it, "the superimposition of a national state, without corresponding transformation of local institutions (or better without an evolution of the spirit of local democracies into national scope) gives us just what we now have in China: A nominal republic governed by a military clique" (MW 11: 212). Many Westerners regarded the 1911 revolution that ended dynastic rule in China as a sure sign of political progress, as a "giant stride out of the nineteenth century into the twentieth century, a move from Asian despotism to western republicanism."[7] Dewey had strong reservations. As he indicated in *The Public and Its Problems*, the Western belief in a model pattern of political development often "flattered the conceit of those [Western] nations which, being politically 'advanced,' assumed that they were so near the apex of evolution as to wear the crown of statehood" (LW 2: 264).

Before Dewey visited China, he had already rejected the supremacy of the state and emphasized instead the emerging reality of transnational interests and organizations. Indeed, Dewey's ideas were always evolving. His observations of international politics and his reflections on the war were sufficient enough to lead him to the same conclusion. However, I maintain that Dewey could not have developed his own account of the state, which appeared in *The Public and Its Problems*, without being informed by his experience in China. In *Reconstruction in Philosophy*, Dewey deplored the fact that traditional political philosophy had been suffering from "abstract definition and ultra-scientific argumentation" (MW 12: 91) and argued that a more scientific, empirical approach was needed for an accurate understanding of the nature of the state. Nonetheless, Dewey lacked a comprehensive historical perspective at the time to allow him to tackle the problem. Fortunately, his two-year visit to China made him acquainted with Chinese history and politics, thereby enabling him to base his inquiry into the state on a wider understanding of concrete, historical facts. This history teaches that no invariant political structures are to be found in the Occident and the Orient in ancient and modern times. From this vantage point, Dewey was able to debunk the Western myth of the state.

Let me conclude this section of the chapter with an additional note. Dewey's call to discard a narrow, fixed metaphysical concept of the state by replacing it with a broad, dynamic experimental concept of the public, presented in the first two chapters of *The Public and Its Problems*, received relatively little attention in the literature, compared to what Dewey said about democracy in the later chapters. In light of the immediate context of U.S. liberalism, Dewey's concerns in these pages may have seemed rather peripheral or remote—if not entirely irrelevant. Those who were concerned merely with U.S. domestic politics might fail to note the relevance of his discussion of the public and the state to his view of democracy in the remainder of the book. However, if we place Dewey's ideas about the public and the state in the larger context of the threat of international war—an ongoing concern of Dewey's—the significance of Dewey's theoretical formulations about the state and the public immediately reveals itself.

In his introduction to the 1942 edition of the book, Dewey reiterated the central point in his analysis of the public and the state. He wrote, "the decline . . . of Isolationism is evidence that there is developing the sense that relations between nations are taking on the properties that constitute a public, and hence call for some measure of political organization" (LW 2: 375). He recapitulated his broader political concern: "The scope, the range, of the public, the question of where the public shall end and the sphere of the private begin, has long been a vital political problem in domestic affairs." He was glad that "At last the same issue is actively raised about the relations between national units, no one of which in the past has acknowledged *political* responsibility in the conduct of its policies toward other national units." He admitted that although "there has been acknowledgment of *moral* responsibility," it broke down very easily in the case of relationships between nations (LW 2: 376). I hope that through my discussion of Dewey's experiences in China in relation to his theory of the public and the state, I have indirectly demonstrated that Dewey had a larger concern in mind than to "save democracy of America" and for America, as one reviewer in the 1920s suggested.[8] Next I discuss the focal point of the book, namely, Dewey's conception of democracy and the influence of China on his matured thinking.

Reconstructing Democracy

Let me begin by addressing the link between Dewey's theory of the public and the state and his conception of democracy. The connection is crucial because it will reveal an important continuity. By debunking the myth of the state and articulating a vision of the public, Dewey forcefully challenges existing political democracies as the best possible states. This in turn enabled him to distinguish between democracy as a system of government and as a way of life. At the same time, this points to the need to reorder political priorities: instead of refining the democratic machinery, we should consolidate and revitalize local communities. If the authoritative aura surrounding the democratic machinery remains unchallenged, democracy as a moral ideal will always elude our attention.

In chapter three of *The Public and Its Problems*, Dewey discussed the emergence of the democratic state in its historical context. Lacking a historical perspective, one tends to make the creation of democracy into a legend, and thus, as Dewey said, to "throw away all means for an intelligent criticism of it." According to the legend, the democratic government originated "in a single clear-cut idea" and proceeded "by a single unbroken impetus to unfold itself to a predestined end." Dewey criticized this view by saying that political movements "do not embody some absolute and unquestioned good." Instead, they "represent a choice, amid a complex of contending forces, of that particular possibility which appears to promise the most good with the least attendant evil" (LW 2: 287). Because democracy as a form of government did not emerge from a clear and potent vision of what democracy is, this lack of a clear vision should propel one to look further into the meaning of democracy rather than to celebrate it with self-congratulatory applauses.

To challenge the sanctity of the political system of democracy, Dewey argued that mechanisms such as universal suffrage, frequent elections, majority rule, the cabinet and congress, should be understood as practical devices "to direct social experimentation," not as "final truths" (LW 2:

326). However, Dewey was aware of the obstacles involved in adopting an experimental approach to politics, namely, our attachments to established norms and values. As he put it, "[e]motional habituations and intellectual habitudes on the part of the mass of men create the conditions of which the exploiters of sentiment and opinion only take advantage." Lamenting the gap between the physical and social sciences' attitudes toward experimentation, Dewey wrote:

> Men have got used to an experimental method in physical and technical matters. They are still afraid of it in human concerns. The fear is the more efficacious because like all deep-lying fears it is covered up and disguised by all kinds of rationalizations. One of its commonest forms is a truly religious idealization of, and reverence for, established institutions; for example in our own politics, the Constitution, the Supreme Court, private property, free contract and so on. (LW 2:341)

Dewey cautioned that the belief in political fixity would lead to stagnation and ultimately revolution.

Even though Dewey seemed rather critical in his attempt to demystify the democratic state and government, he acknowledged a steady historical current in the direction of political governance "toward democratic forms." As he observed, "That government exists to serve its community, and that this purpose cannot be achieved unless the community itself shares in selecting its governors and determining their policies, are a deposit of fact left . . . permanently in the wake of doctrines and forms, however transitory the latter." Therefore, he thought it reasonable to expect that "whatever changes may take place in existing democratic machinery, they will be of a sort to make the interest of the public a more supreme guide and criterion of governmental activity, and to enable the public to form and manifest its purposes still more authoritatively" (LW 2: 327). Nonetheless, Dewey insisted that this expressed only the political phase of democracy.

Dewey believed that the cure for the ills of democracy is more democracy—not in the sense of more machinery, but in the sense of a fuller grasp of the idea. Democracy will be secured only when we discover the means by which a scattered public can organize itself and express its interests. Dewey also claimed that "this discovery is necessarily precedent to any fundamental change in the machinery." It is "somewhat futile" to consider what forms of political machinery are best as long as we remain at the stage of "the Great Society," rather than that of "the Great Community" (LW 2: 327). If a flourishing, functioning community exists, the problems of political machinery will not be particularly pressing or predominant. Discussions of and solutions to these problems will be integrated into the daily lives of people in their communities as they gather for social events or formal meetings. Political democracy in its narrow sense does not affect all modes of human association, which include, for instance, the family, the school, the workplace, and the temple or church. Therefore, it offers little assistance in creating cohesive communities. Dewey said that important questions concerning the well-being of communities were practical matters, such as transportation, public health, city planning, regulation of immigrants, adjustment of taxation, and preparation of teachers. He asked, "What has counting heads, decision by majority and the whole apparatus of traditional government to do with such things?" Dewey said that the assumed public represented by the political machinery of democracy is "not only a ghost, but a ghost which walks and talks, and obscures, confuses and misleads governmental action in a disastrous way" (LW 2: 313).

The central contention of *The Public and Its Problems* lies in this often-quoted line in which Dewey proclaimed, "regarded as an idea, democracy is not an alternative to other principles of associated life. It is the idea of community life itself." As he elaborated:

> Wherever there is conjoint activity whose consequences are appreciated as good by all singular persons who take part in it, and where the realization of the good is such as to effect an energetic desire and effort to sustain it in being just because it is a good shared by all, there is in so far a community. The clear consciousness of a communal life, in all its implications, constitutes the idea of democracy. (LW 2: 328)

This moral vision of democracy as an ideal community is surely inspiring. However, Dewey was not proposing a utopian dream; he said that democracy in this sense "is not a fact and never will be" (LW 2: 328). Nevertheless, he urged that we start from a firmer grasp of the ideal community life against which to measure our cherished norms, values, and customs to better propel our future more reliably toward this goal.

Dewey redefined the meaning of liberty and equality in the context of community life. Liberty, he said, does not mean "independence of social ties," as in the sense of absolute autonomy. Liberty is what secures "release and fulfillment of personal potentialities which take place only in rich and manifold association with others." It is "the power to be an individualized self making a distinctive contribution and enjoying in its own way the fruits of association." Equality, Dewey noted, does not signify some kind of "mathematical or physical equivalence in virtue of which any one element may be substituted for another." Rather, it "denotes the unhampered share with which each individual member of the community has in the consequences of associated action" as well as an "effective regard for whatever is distinctive and unique in each, irrespective of physical and psychological inequalities" (LW 2: 329–30). Equality is not a "natural possession," but "a fruit of community." To counter the ingrained individualism in the Western intellectual tradition, Dewey said, "To learn to be human is to develop through the give-and-take of communication an effective sense of being an individually distinctive member of a community; one who understands and appreciates its beliefs, desires, and methods, and who contributes to a further conversion of organic powers into human resources and values" (LW 2: 332). In rejecting the notion of the discrete individual and affirming the role of community in creating individuals, Dewey proposed a vision of democracy that diverges greatly from the rights-based liberalism of much Western political thought. I return to this point in the final section of this chapter.

Now let me compare Dewey's *Democracy and Education* with his *The Public and Its Problems* to show the nuanced but substantial differences in Dewey's treatment of democracy. In the former, Dewey wrote that democracy is "primarily a mode of associated living, of conjoint communicated experience" (MW 9: 93). However, the associated living does not guarantee communicated experience. People can be associated in many ways without feeling a sense of connectedness to one another and having a clear understanding of one another. In the latter, Dewey called attention to the insufficiency of mere association by saying, "No amount of aggregated collective action of itself constitutes a community." Dewey further differentiated associated living from communal life: "Association itself is physical and organic while communal life is moral, that is emotionally, intellectually, consciously sustained" (LW 2: 330). In Dewey's view, "we are born organic beings associated with others, but we are not born members of a community" (LW 2: 331). Associated living is not a sufficient condition of democracy as a form of community life that Dewey later emphasized.

In *Democracy and Education*, Dewey explicitly claimed, "a democracy is more than a form of government." Nonetheless, he used the example of a despotically governed state—a political example—as a contrast to democracy. He took pains to explain how such a state failed to meet his democratic criterion: namely, the number and variety of interests shared and the fullness of interplay between various social groups. Even though Dewey sensed the insufficiency of the political connotations of democracy, he was unable to remove democracy from its political ancestry. The Western political heritage still had a hold on him. Furthermore, Dewey's critique of despotism may be easily taken to imply that no democracy exists in a despotically governed state. This may be the case with the relationship between the ruler and the ruled. However, in the relationships among individuals in their local environments where imperial power hardly ever reaches, "conjoint and communicated experiences" may be common and frequent.

Dewey later seemed to have sensed the inadequacy of his earlier presupposition. Therefore, he made a small but important qualification when writing *The Public and Its Problems.* In describing the premodern forms of human association, such as those Chinese village life represents, Dewey wrote:

> Those [associations] which were important, which really counted in forming emotional and intellectual dispositions, were local and contiguous and consequently visible. Human beings, if they shared in them at all, shared directly and in a way of which they were aware in both their affections and their beliefs. The state, *even when it despotically interfered,* was remote, an agency alien to daily life. Otherwise it entered men's lives through custom and common law. (LW 2: 295–96, emphasis added)

Dewey seemed to realize that one can be easily prejudiced by the political appearance of a despotic state without looking into its people's ordinary ways of life that may be harmonious and democratic. Dewey later accentuated the fact that democracy is "a complex affair" and that its different meanings and ramifications need to be thoroughly clarified (LW 2: 287).

Having briefly outlined the development in Dewey's thinking about democracy by comparing two of his major works, I would like to elaborate on the theme by referring to the larger corpus of Dewey's works in the early, middle, and later periods to show that throughout his life, Dewey continuously revised and reconstructed his conception of democracy in light of new experiences, new circumstances, and new challenges. I also show that Dewey's visit to China marks an important turning point in his long and arduous journey toward an inspiring vision of democracy that is political as well as ethical, local as well as global. My central contention is that his encounter with China reinforced his belief in the essential value of community life for democracy.

Before I start the discussion, I would like to acknowledge the important fact that the differentiation between democracy as government and as way of life had been consistently present throughout Dewey's voluminous writings, including his early essays. For instance, in "The Ethics of Democracy" (1888), Dewey argued that to conceive of democracy merely as a form of government is "like saying that home is more or less [a] geometrical arrangement of bricks and mortar." Democracy "is a form of government only because it is a form of moral and spiritual association" (EW 1: 240). Despite this caveat, the distinction was most clearly and thoroughly expounded in *The Public and Its Problems*, the significance of which should not be overlooked.

In Dewey's 1927 rendition of democracy as the idea of community life, one perceives an unprecedented concreteness and clarity of thought, compared with his earlier remarks about democracy, which were relatively abstract. In "The Ethics of Democracy" Dewey wrote, "Democracy approaches most nearly the ideal of all social organization; that in which the individual and society are organic to each other." As noted, in *Democracy and Education*, Dewey defined democracy as "a mode of associated living, of conjoint communicated experience" (MW 9: 93). In *Reconstruction in Philosophy*, Dewey interpreted the moral meaning of democracy as suggesting that "the supreme test of all political institutions and industrial arrangements shall be the contribution they make to the all-around growth of every member of society" (MW 12: 186). In *The Public and Its Problems*, Dewey pinned down the meaning of democracy as ideal community life: "the clear consciousness of a communal life, in all its manifestations, constitutes the idea of democracy" (LW 2: 328). Dewey further interpreted the meanings of fraternity, liberty, and equality in connection with communal life.

Apart from the apparent concreteness in his 1927 rendition of democracy, the slight change of emphasis in wording from associative-communicative living to communal life is itself revealing. Communal life better captures the emotional and aesthetic dimensions of human association and interaction needed to sustain a genuine democracy. This is to say that a genuine democratic way of life is impossible without a sense of togetherness and oneness experienced and appreciated by its participants. Even though Dewey's commitment to the importance of community life was already present in his early writings, the question arises why Dewey did not link the idea of democracy directly with the idea of community until he wrote *The Public and Its Problems*. Let us turn to his experiences in China to illuminate our answers.

We may start by considering Dewey's exposure to Chinese social life and political psychology. As he described:

> The actual government of China was a system of nicely calculated personal and group pressures and pulls, exactions and "squeezes," neatly balanced against one another, of assertions and yieldings, of experiments to see how far a certain demand could be forced, and of yielding when the exorbitance of the demand called out an equal counter-pressure. Long before the time of Sir Isaac Newton, China worked out a demonstration in the field of politics, of the law that action and reaction are equal and in opposite directions. It exemplified the working of the principle in every aspect of human association. (MW 11: 219)

Dewey admired the Chinese social system and said that it "implies a high state of civilization" and "produces civilized persons almost automatically" (MW 11: 220). As he explained, the essence of civility "is the ability to live consciously along with others, aware of their expectations, demands and rights, of the pressure they can put upon one, while also conscious of just how far one can go in response in exerting pressure upon others." Dewey praised the Chinese for figuring out "all the complex elements of the social equation" with "unparalleled exactness." He claimed, "Their social calculus, integral and differential, exceeded anything elsewhere in existence" (MW 11: 220).

In addition, Dewey was also impressed by the "law-abidingness" of the Chinese people, despite the absence of a sound legal system. He wrote:

> If you read the books written about China, you find the Chinese often spoken of as the "most law-abiding people in the world." Struck by this fact, the traveler often neglects to go behind it. He fails to note that this law-abidingness constantly shows itself in contempt for everything that we in the West associate with law, that it goes on largely without courts, without legal and judicial forms and officers; that, in fact, the Chinese regularly do what the West regards as the essence of lawlessness—enforce the law through private agencies and arrangements. In many things the one who is regarded as breaking the real law, the controlling custom, is the one who appeals to the "law"—that is, to governmental agencies and officers. (MW 12: 41)

As Dewey further commented, "To western eyes, accustomed to the forms of regular hearings and trials, such a method seems lawless. In China, however, the moral sense of the community would have been shocked by a purely legal treatment" (MW 12: 42). Dewey understood "this seeming absence of public law" as meaning that "troubles of importance are regarded as between groups, and to be settled between them and by their own initiative" (MW 12: 43). Obviously, Dewey did not approve of complete reliance on the legal system to maintain social harmony. Instead, he preferred moral persuasion in the natural setting of communal life. In China, where "the sphere of discretion will always be large in contrast with that of set forms," Western legalism, as Dewey said, "will be short-circuited." When commenting on a new trend in China toward establishing Western systems of law, Dewey actually hoped that China would not "make the complete surrender to legalism and formalism that western nations have done"—which would be "one of the contributions of China to the world" (MW 12: 47).

Moreover, what impressed Dewey the most about the Chinese is their community of life. As he commented:

What the Chinese abundantly possess is community of life, a sense of unity of civilization, of immemorial continuity of customs and ideals. The consciousness of a unity of pattern woven through the whole fabric of their existence never leaves them. To be a Chinese is not to be of a certain race nor to yield allegiance to a certain national state. It is to share with countless millions of others in certain ways of feeling and thinking, fraught with innumerable memories and expectations because of long-established modes of adjustment and intercourse. (MW 11: 223)

The sense of community life brought about by shared culture struck Dewey as a marvelous achievement. In the example of the Chinese, Dewey saw that the solidarity of shared culture itself, independent of a strong central state or effective political machinery, has the power to unite its people and to cultivate a sense of community, despite differences in ethnicity and religion.

The Chinese sense of connection to each other, as opposed to independence and detachment from one another, impressed Dewey greatly. In his constant fight against the rugged individualism in the Western intellectual tradition, Dewey aimed to promote a more community-oriented culture in which people would pride themselves not only in being autonomous individuals, but also in being distinctive members of a community. This is a culture in which people embrace interpersonal interaction and communication as providing opportunities for intellectual and moral growth, rather than as obstructing possibilities for self-realization. Dewey understood the fact that as a nation composed of people from all over the world, the United States was faced with a unique challenge to establish a sense of cultural solidarity and social unity, which is intellectually, emotionally, and morally sustained, rather than politically imposed. Dewey's philosophy, especially in the late 1920s, can be seen as an attempt to direct Americans' thinking about democracy toward this vision. His direct exposure to Chinese culture, as it was embodied in the day-to-day living of the masses, deepened his understanding of the fundamental value of communal life, which was not abundantly expressed nor widely acknowledged in the predominantly individualistic culture of the modern West.

To debunk the myth of an autonomous, presocial self, Dewey insisted that "everything which is distinctively human is learned, not native" (LW 2: 331). The sense of self, rather than arriving at birth, is to be gradually developed in the immediate family and the surrounding community to which one is born. Unfortunately, the dominant conception of the self as a product rather than a process represents a gross distortion of the human condition. To push the trend of thinking more toward communitarian perspectives, Dewey suggested that we emphasize the traits of human association and communication that are distinctively human, those by which "each acts, in so far as the connection is known, in view of the connection" to others. Interconnectedness, rather than independence, is the keynote of a conscious moral life. Even though "individuals still do the thinking, desiring and purposing," what they think and desire is "the consequences of their behavior upon that of others and that of others upon themselves" (LW 2: 250).

In fact, even though our habits, beliefs, interests, and values are individually owned, they are largely shaped by interpersonal contacts, knowingly or unknowingly. I visited a local museum in a small Midwestern town with a special exhibition displaying the private collections of neighborhood schoolchildren. Each display window had a personal letter written by the collector to explain how he or she started the collection. Most of them wrote that their interests in collecting travel souvenirs, fishing equipment, or even the caps of milk containers came from the influence of family members, who either started the collection or encouraged them to do so and helped them along the way. This example illustrates the inevitable social origins of our personal interests, habits, and values that fundamentally make up who we are—even though we are ultimately individual and unique. As Dewey put it succinctly, "for beings who observe and think, and whose ideas are absorbed by impulses and become sentiments and interests, 'we' is inevitable as 'I'" (LW 2: 330).

Indeed, whether we like it or not, we are invariably interconnected and interdependent, and the more we are aware of the fact and attend to it, the more we are able to live a moral life. For Dewey, human interconnection is not a shackle to escape. On the contrary, he accepts the fact, affirms it, and embraces it because it furnishes the ground for development and growth. Unlike those who regard human sociality as an obstacle to individual autonomy, Dewey celebrates personal uniqueness as growing out of the context of social interaction and communication. Dewey once commented negatively about the notion of self-reliance, noting "there is always a danger that increased personal independence will decrease the social capacity of an individual." As he cautioned, "in making him more self-reliant, it may make him more self-sufficient; it may lead to aloofness and indifference. It often makes an individual so insensitive in his relations to others as to develop an illusion of being really able to stand and act alone." Dewey called this "an unnamed form of insanity which is responsible for a large part of the remediable suffering of the world" (MW 9: 49).

The communal feature of Chinese life convinced Dewey that China possessed the foundation on which Chinese democracy was to be based. As far as China's current crisis and future were concerned, he suggested that the road to transformation and modernization be based on a further-ing of its indigenous democratic practices and spirit rather than direct copying of Western democracy.

> The promise of China's rebirth into full membership in the modern world is found in its democratic habits of life and thought, provided we add to the statement another: the peculiar quality of this democ-racy also forms the strongest obstacle to the making over of China in its confrontation by a waiting, restless and greedy world. For while China is morally and intellectually a democracy of a paternalistic type, she lacks the specific organs by which alone a democracy can effectively sustain itself either internally or internationally. China is in a dilemma whose seriousness can hardly be exaggerated. Her ha-bitual decentralization, her centrifugal localisms, operate against her becoming a nationalistic entity with the institutions of public reve-nue, unitary public order, defense, legislation and diplomacy that are imperatively needed. Yet her deepest traditions, her most established ways of feeling and thinking, her essential democracy, cluster about the local units, the village and its neighbors. (MW 11: 212)

Dewey criticized the prevailing tendency in "Western thought" that "con-fined itself to the more obvious, the more structural, factors of the prob-lem." These problems such as "the adjustment of the power and author-ity of the central government to that of local and regional governments," "the relations of the executive and legislative forces in the government," "the revision of legal procedure and law to eliminate arbitrariness and personal discretion"—all of these, Dewey argued, were peripheral to the real problem of China. The real problem is "how the democratic spirit historically manifest in the absence of classes, the prevalence of social and civil equality, the control of individuals and groups by moral rather than physical force—that is, by instruction, advice, and public opinion rather than definitive legal methods—can find an organized expression of itself" (LW 2: 212–13).

To borrow Dewey's own wording in *The Public and Its Problems,* which bears some similarity to what he wrote here, the real problem of China is that its inchoate, democratic public needs to identify and organize itself. Dewey's hope for Young China is that in its vigorous attempt to break with the past to transform itself, it will preserve its essential democracy, which he once described as "social" (MW 13: 230). Chinese social and communal life—despite its lack of a democratic government—points to the potentiality for a social form of democracy to stimulate political change. Dewey's visit to China gave him the op-portunity to cast aside the political baggage of the West and to witness an inchoate form of democracy in the absence of all the political, legal contrivances so endearing to the Western mind. This experience highlighted the fundamental contribution of community life to creating and sustaining democracy. In his response to the criticisms Lippmann raised against political democracy, Dewey felt compelled to press on the issue of the distinction between democracy as government and as community life, and accordingly, to reconstruct his conception of democracy, as informed by his experiences in China.

The two meanings of democracy are definitely related because "the idea remains barren and empty save as it is incarnated in human relationship"—which, of course, includes the way people select government officials to represent their interests. (LW 2: 325). In making the differentiation, Dewey did not mean to establish an arbitrary dualism he fought his entire life. Nonetheless, the two phases of democracy needed to be separated in discussion in that "the idea of democracy is a wider and fuller idea than can be exemplified in the state even at its best." As J. Tiles aptly contends, Dewey took democracy to encompass "a form of culture."[9] Politics is only one aspect of culture, albeit an important one. For democracy to become an all-encompassing culture, it must affect all modes of human association. For all modes of human association to be affected, the consolidation of local communities is the surer road to success. In a flourishing, functioning community, political problems are a part of the daily process of learning to live along with others, to work with others, and to solve problems together.

In his intellectual biography of Dewey, Robert Westbrook notes that "a familiar impatience crept into Dewey's discussion of the institutions of political democracy in *The Public and Its Problems,* as if somehow consideration of such matters was really beside the point or at least not properly at the heart of a democratic philosophy."[10] Westbrook's observation captures Dewey's overall feeling that U.S. democracy had been too externalized and politicized and that it needed to be more internalized and socialized. Even though the social conditions in U.S. society at the time undoubtedly propelled Dewey to prioritize social over political democracy, Dewey's experiences in China helped reinforce his essential faith in democracy as a form of culture that fosters community life. This faith, once tested and consolidated, remained consistent throughout his later career.

In *Liberalism and Social Action* (1935), Dewey identified the problem of democracy as that of "[forming] social organization, extending to all the areas and ways of living, in which the powers of individuals shall not be merely released from mechanical external constraint but shall be fed, sustained and directed" (LW 11: 25). He meant that the individual capacities and powers required for democracy should be internally maintained by the nutrients of a flourishing, communal life. In *Freedom* and Culture (1939), Dewey noted again this difference between "a society, in the sense of an association, and a community." He argued that associations are basic "conditions for the existence of a community, but a community adds the function of communication in which emotions and ideas are shared as well as joint undertaking engaged in" (LW 13: 176). In this book, Dewey quoted a passage from his earlier *The Public and Its Problems*, reminding his readers again that democracy must begin at the neighborly community.

Dewey summed up his faith in democracy in a short essay, "Creative Democracy—The Task before Us" (1939), written for his eightieth birthday celebration. Dewey expressed his conviction that democracy is "a personal, an individual, way of life" (LW 14: 226). Dewey urged us to "get rid of the habit of thinking of democracy as something institutional and external" and "to acquire the habit of treating it as a way of personal life" to realize democracy as a moral ideal (LW 14: 228). Democracy as a way of life signifies "the possession and continual use of certain attitudes, forming personal character and determining desire and purpose in all the relations of life," and thus it cannot be "separated from individual attitudes so deep-seated as to constitute character" (LW 14: 226). This is to say that the hope of realizing democracy as a commonplace of living depends on the character of each member in society. Dewey's eloquent description of a democratic character is worth quoting at length:

> [D]emocracy as a way of life is controlled by personal faith in personal day-by-day working together with others. Democracy is the belief that even when needs and ends or consequences are different for each individual, the habit of amicable cooperation—which may include, as in sport, rivalry and competition—is itself a priceless addition to life. To take as far as possible every conflict which arises—and they are bound to arise—out of the atmosphere and medium of force, of violence as a means of settlement into that of discussion and of intelligence is to treat those who disagree—even profoundly—with us as those from whom we may learn, and in so far, as friends. . . . To cooperate by giving differences a chance to show themselves because of the belief that the expression of difference is not only a right of the other persons [sic] but is a means of enriching one's own life-experience, is inherent in the democratic personal way of life. (LW 14: 228)

By insisting that the democratic way of life is ultimately personal, Dewey did not mean that it is a life independent of social ties or a life in isolation from others. Life in isolation is rather a danger to be avoided because it hampers the development of a democratic, moral character. As Dewey contended in *Ethics* (1932), "The kind of self formed through action faithful to relations with others will be a fuller and broader self than one cultivated in isolation from or in opposition to the purposes and needs of others" (LW 7: 302). The democratic character Dewey envisioned can be developed and cultivated only through the ordinary rhythms of a communal life. In fact, the emphasis in democracy as constituted in personal, moral character echoes what Dewey wrote in his 1888 essay, "The Ethics of Democracy," in which he claimed that "democracy means that personality is the first and final reality"—except that his earlier statement was relatively abstract and difficult to comprehend in a world wholly preoccupied with political democracy (EW 1: 240).

Translated into a philosophical position, democracy as a way of life is grounded in the faith that "the process of experience is capable of being educative, [and] faith in democracy is all one with faith in experience and education" (LW 14: 229). To borrow the terminology from *Democracy and Education,* faith in experience and education means faith in education as growth, which signifies a process of living that "has no end beyond itself," but is its own end of "continual reorganizing, reconstructing, transforming" (MW 9: 54). Democracy as a moral ideal is determined by what each of us learns from our experiences of living among others and with others—with those we love or hate and with whom we agree or disagree, with those we spend a lifetime or meet only once. The hope of democracy as a moral ideal lies in the personal character of the people themselves—in whether they are cooperative or competitive, amicable or antagonistic, inquiring or dogmatic, open-minded or narrow-minded.

To lead a democratic way of life is an art. As Sor-hoon Tan notes, the connection of Dewey's social philosophy and his aesthetics has often been neglected.[11] In *Art as Experience* (1934), Dewey explained how we are able to transform our ordinary experiences in the normal process of living into consummatory, aesthetic experiences that make life worth living. The democratic character Dewey envisages requires the courage not to avoid interpersonal problems or social disputes due to differences of opinion and conflicts of interest, but to accept them as natural rhythms of life, like the ebbing and flowing of the sea. As Dewey said, "we envisage with pleasure Nirvana and a uniform heavenly bliss only because they are projected upon the background of our present world of stress and conflict." He warned, "Where everything is already complete, there is no fulfillment." Because the actual world in which we live is "a combination of movement and culmination, of breaks and re-unions, the experience of a living creature is capable of esthetic quality" (LW 10: 22). In the process of losing and reestablishing harmony with our surroundings, we are living the most intense and worthwhile life, Dewey said. The art of democratic living lies in the joint undertaking to transform disorderly experiences into harmonious ones that allow every participant involved the opportunity to grow. The kind of creative intelligence and aesthetic sensibility required to turn narrowness into openness, shallowness into depth, and conflict into harmony, has to be developed through the process of living a conscious, mindful life. Consummatory, aesthetic experiences are conducive to personal happiness and social well-being and are attainable at all levels of human interaction throughout all stages of life—if one's mind and heart are set for learning. This learning was clearly exemplified in the life of Dewey himself.

When Dewey was writing in the 1930s, he lamented, "much of the intimate social connection is lost in the impersonality of a world market" (LW 10: 15). In today's technological culture, the problem is even worse. Although new information technologies have created expedient ways of association and communication, they do not guarantee genuine and meaningful exchange of ideas and feelings among people. In fact, one can easily create an illusory safe haven in the world of the Internet, avoiding contact with real people, escaping from interpersonal problems, and leading a life utterly alientated from others. Consequently, families scatter and decline; communities dissolve. Economic prosperity and political stability have allowed many of us to become our own persons and to lead our own lives free from political oppression or religious prosecution. But what kind of persons we become and what kind of lives we choose to lead depend largely on the culture in which we live. The question is: Is our culture conducive or inimical to democracy?

Having elaborated on the development in Dewey's thinking about democracy as a moral ideal, I would like to return to the theme of Dewey's visit to China and the significance of this encounter. In some sense, Dewey's shift of emphasis from democracy as government to democracy as culture represents a Copernican revolution in Western political thinking. In his attempt to clarify the relationship between politics and culture, Dewey was reversing a common assumption about the progress of civilization: namely, that well-designed political machinery will lead to a democratic form of culture. Rather, Dewey wanted to argue that the creation of democracy as a form of culture and as a personal way of life will gradually lead to better answers to the question of political governance. In a nutshell, the American philosopher of democracy traveled to China and was reinforced in his belief that democracy is first and foremost an all-encompassing culture. Perhaps Dewey could not have reached this conclusion or felt so confident about it if he had not encountered China.

Mapping Out a Future for Confucian Democracy

Hearing Dewey describe China as democratic—even if this only means that it possesses the cultural and social preconditions for democracy—may be disorienting and disconcerting. The statement may shake the presumptions of Western political leaders who had been, and are still, try-ing to impose democracy on nations that do not embrace Western liber-alism. The presumed opposition between Chinese authoritarianism and Western liberalism is so deeply ingrained in the popular conceptions of the Western world that imagining a democratic China is difficult. To rec-ognize and acknowledge China's indigenous form of democracy, which operates under a very different trajectory than that in the West, requires an open mind and a far-reaching insight. The "particular direction" of China's democracy deserves a more precise label than what Dewey only vaguely calls "social" democracy, namely, "Confucian democracy."

Initially the notion of Confucian democracy may seem like "a con-tradiction in terms," as Harvard professor Samuel Huntington claimed; Huntington thinks that the Confucian emphasis on "the group over the individual, authority over liberty, and responsibility over rights," along with its lack of "a tradition of rights against the state," make traditional Confucianism "either undemocratic or antidemocratic."[12] However, if we try to distinguish Confucian political regimes from Confucian ways of life as the scholar of Confucianism Tu Wei-ming suggests, we can move from "political Confucianism" as the remnant of the past to a future of Confu-cianism that is full of hope and constructive possibilities.[13] For a brighter future, we must abandon "the great meta-narrative of enlightenment and modernity" as nothing more than a "provincial myth."[14] We should re-member that democratic institutions in Europe emerged from historically tyrannical, hierarchical, and authoritarian cultures. As Edward Friedman notes, unless one can show that Confucian culture "foster[s] obstacles to democracy greater than those undergirded [by] Robespierre, Mussolini, Franco, and Hitler," one has no reason to deny the possibility of Confu-cian democracy in China.

However, ethnocentric pride and self-complacency make it easy to insist on a single, liberal model of democracy and to disregard "Asian-style" democracy as a myth—a form of soft authoritarianism that has "not yet completed the transition to democracy."[15] In fact, no singular democ-racy exists even in the West, as Friedman reminds us. Where democracy has traveled, we have seen successful cases of creative borrowing. "In every locale (and in every theoretical construct), people struggle to trans-late a traveling theory to accommodate their own ongoing experiences, imperatives, and tensions. The momentary synthesis and the transitory uniqueness are ubiquitous." Actually, with regard to principles and pro-cesses of democratization, the divide between the West and the non-West is only expedient. As Friedman contends, "All cultures can accommodate democracy. Each can learn from all the rest because each is unique at the same time all have much in common. Each nation must craft a democracy to suit its own historical and societal particulars."[16]

To craft a democracy to suit the Confucian culture of China, David Hall and Roger Ames have propagated and promoted the notion of "Confucian democracy" in their pioneering work, *Democracy of the Dead: Dewey, Confucius and the Hope of Democracy for China* (1999). In this book, they remind readers, "China has always been, and will continue to be, a communitarian society and that accommodating the legitimate desires of the Chinese people requires the promotion of a communitarian form of democracy seriously at odds with the liberal model that presently dominates Western democracies." They argue that Dewey's vision of democracy as ideal community life is "best suited to engage the realities and Chinese social practice and to support the realization of a 'Confucian democracy' in China."[17] They further contend that Confucian democracy is more congenial to Dewey's understanding than typical liberal models of democracy. Indeed, for the idea of Confucian democracy to gain recognition, we need to alter our conception of democracy and clarify our misunderstandings about Confucianism. In *Confucian Democracy: A Deweyan Reconstruction* (2003), Sor-hoon Tan examines the commonalities between classical Confucianism and Deweyan pragmatism. She holds that a synthesis of their philosophies can offer an alternative to Western liberal models of democracy. Indeed, this new scholarship on Dewey and Confucius has aroused a considerable degree of scholarly attention and interest. The following discusses the implications of my work for Confucian democracy, which will redirect our thinking about the future of democracy for both China and the United States and facilitate a thoughtful and mutually respectful dialogue between the two nations.

To begin with, some of Dewey's own observations and appraisals of Chinese society can give credence to the legitimacy of a communitarian form of democracy for China. Take, for example, the fact that Dewey perceived great merit in the way Chinese traditionally resolve social conflict—namely, not through public laws but through personal initiatives and social rituals. As noted, Dewey found that Western legal methods of dispute resolution offended Chinese sensibilities. Inherent in the Chinese rejection of such legal remedies is a fundamental respect for moral cultivation. Dewey described this particular characteristic of Chinese society as embodying a democratic spirit and hoped that the Chinese would preserve their cultural strength while adapting to modern requirements of legalism—and this, he added, would be "one of China's contributions to the world" (MW 12: 47).

Dewey's endorsement marks an example of his divergence from rights-based liberalism and of his affinities with Confucianism. Liberalism sanctions reliance on impersonal government agencies to protect rights and enforce justice. However, Dewey's democratic theory values the immediate and ongoing process of interpersonal communication, negotiation, and moral persuasion. Through this interactive process, people are more likely to learn to understand the needs and perspectives of others, to modify their actions according to perceived consequences for others, and to pursue interests and goals held in common. By contrast, the legal system does not aim to enhance communication and understanding. Serving sentences and paying fines do not necessarily make people take responsibility or feel remorse about their acts. Law uses coercion and fear but does not appeal to or foster loftier feelings and aspirations. For both Dewey and Confucius, genuine consensus should be "achieved at the aesthetic and practical level not merely through claims of reason."[18]

The Chinese attitude toward the law reflects an influence of Confucius's insistence on the priority of morality over law. As Tan says, "Confucius was distrustful of relying on what he called 'guiding the people by edict, and keeping them in line with punishments'—that is, depending on specific laws—as a grounding for social order, because law does not respect the need for virtue."[19] Confucius understood that one cannot rely on the rule of law to bring about a well-ordered and harmonious community and that the key to a flourishing community lies in educating people through rituals rather than punishing them through laws. Apart from these philosophical implications, the difference in the conception of law has a deeper historical root. As Hall and Ames's analysis shows, law develops in Confucian China "to articulate administrative duties and to overcome deficiencies of ritual in maintaining social stability," whereas "in the West, law originates as a response to despotic power" and "functions to protect the individual citizen against the state, and against the tyranny of the majority." Therefore, law is important in the West because it aims to protect individual rights, whereas in the Confucian social system, resorting to law is "denigrated as a sign of the failure of ritual to achieve social harmony—especially a *moral* failure."[20]

Like Dewey, Confucius values the educative function of community life and is "committed to the fundamental importance of proximate, self-invested relationships."[21] As Hall and Ames point out, Confucius "sees a thriving, self-governing community, achieved through mediating institutions such as family and neighborhood, as the optimum guarantee of a personal liberty and the best opportunity for full participation in a shared vision of community." The Confucian model of democracy places a high premium on the goal of self-ordering and hence avoids fear and coercion as means of sustaining social order. Instead, it "depends upon the powerful informal pressures of shame (*chi*) and the personalization of deferential roles and relations (*li*) as its motive forces."[22] In this respect, Chinese communities requires "a minimum of formally constituted government" because "the same communal harmony that defines and dispenses order at the most immediate level is relied upon to focus authoritative consensus."[23] During his stay in China, Dewey was quite impressed by the Confucian social system, saying that it represented a "Newtonian" achievement in the course of human history. As noted earlier, he described it as a highly calibrated system of countervailing social pressures (MW 11: 220). Dewey clearly valued this balanced process of interpersonal push and pull as representing a clear consciousness of communal life. What he had witnessed may be regarded as the success of the Confucian project to "create a community as an extended family," as Hall and Ames put it.[24]

Most important, Dewey's social conception of the person makes him more Confucian than liberal. Typical liberal philosophers insist on the concept of the atomized individual, self-defining and self-governing. Dewey disagrees with this notion of individuality and would agree with Tan that "human existence is an 'embedded' phenomenon, depending more on traditional, communal, and inherited meanings than individualistic ones."[25] To become fully human means being fully situated in one's natural, social, and cultural surroundings; it "involves benefiting and being benefited by membership in a world of reciprocal loyalties and obligations which stimulate one, and help to define one's own worth."[26] This is a model of a human coming into being rather than simply being. What classical Confucianism presents is a conception of personhood as a contingent process. As Henry Rosemont observes, "for the early Confucians there can be no 'me' in isolation, to be considered abstractly: I am the totality of the roles I live in relation to specific others." In some ways, saying "I 'play' or 'perform' these roles" is misleading; the truth is that "I am my roles."[27] However, to say that our individuality is largely conferred on us, as we contribute to conferring it on others, is not to deny the uniqueness of every individual. On the contrary, it is to affirm the very uniqueness of each person because no two persons can have the same experiences throughout their lives; even if they theoretically can, they do not perceive the same experiences the same way.

The processive notion of person that defines Confucianism at its core can mitigate the effects of communal hierarchy.[28] Both the person and the community in classical Confucianism are horizontal concepts. Russell Fox argues, "Through ritual activity, everyone holds to their roles, and everyone, in different times and places, has the potential to show forth, through their participation in community activities, the sort of authority which binds the community together." He adds, "The fact that Confucianism has over the centuries supported hierarchical governments that have ignored this ethical and moral perspective is tragic and beside the point of what Confucius and his disciples actually wrote."[29] In fact, a Confucian community is "relatively decentralized and makes few demands; its leaders, however arrived at, are to be concerned with their moral and ritual roles, not the particular activities of every member of the community."[30] The Confucian notion of authority is always moral and aesthetic. The authority of the ruler derives from following the example of virtue as rule is exercised.[31]

Tan further makes the argument that an ideal Confucian community sanctions a "differentiated" but not hierarchical order. As she explains, "this is not to deny that ranking . . . is part of the differentiation required in such a community. What it denies is that such ranking has to be so totalistic that if one is superior, one is superior always and in all things." Moreover, this ranking does not have to be "so inflexible that one is born into a fixed place in the rigid social order and must live one's life as prescribed by one's position with no possibility of change."[32] Despite differences in ranking, everyone in a Confucian democracy is unique and equal. The democratic notion of equality is not to be understood mathematically—everyone having the same things or having the same amount of something—but rather as a qualitative concept, namely, "the equality of opportunity for growth," as Tan aptly suggests.[33]

Hall and Ames have written that "democracy, as the ideal of community life, follows different rhythms and time schedules in different cultural environments . . . . [W]ere we to look at China with John Dewey's democracy in mind, our vision might be transformed."[34] Because many of the claims they make about the commonalities between Confucianism and Dewey's vision of democracy are actually in keeping with Dewey's own observations and appraisals of China, the case that Dewey's own vision was influenced by his encounter with China is strengthened. For this reason, Hall and Ames may be quite right in concluding, "in any future engagements, it may well be the influence of China that brings the United States and other North Atlantic democracies closer to Dewey's democratic vision."[35]

CHAPTER 6

CONTINUING THE DIALOGUE ON
DEWEY AND CHINA

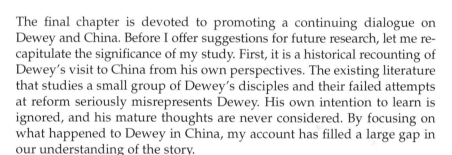

The final chapter is devoted to promoting a continuing dialogue on Dewey and China. Before I offer suggestions for future research, let me recapitulate the significance of my study. First, it is a historical recounting of Dewey's visit to China from his own perspectives. The existing literature that studies a small group of Dewey's disciples and their failed attempts at reform seriously misrepresents Dewey. His own intention to learn is ignored, and his mature thoughts are never considered. By focusing on what happened to Dewey in China, my account has filled a large gap in our understanding of the story.

On another level, my book is a detailed analysis of the intriguing dynamics involved in the encounter between Dewey and modern Chinese intellectuals. By examining their critical responses to Dewey, my study reveals that their own vexed interests largely determined how they perceived and appropriated Dewey's ideas. By exploring what Dewey learned in China, I show that the intellectual exchange was not a one-way street. Dewey's experiences in China helped him better understand international politics and enabled him to review his social and political philosophy in a fresh light.

Finally, my book combines biography with philosophy, providing a rare glimpse of Dewey enacting his own ideas—his pragmatic sensibilities and democratic ideals that were often expressed only abstractly. My study also helps us understand an important tendency in Dewey's later philosophy, namely, his growing sensitivity to the role of culture in shaping human conduct and institutions. His learning about Chinese society

121

and culture contributed to an expansion of his philosophy—hitherto reflecting only Western examples and experiences. Dewey's visit to Japan and China, along with his subsequent international travels, had transformed him from a U.S. philosopher into a transnational one.

Dewey was obviously thinking ahead of his time. Even though he was never a great prophet, he was a remarkable philosopher whose concerns and ideas still remain relevant and important. His appreciation for the latent roots of democracy in Chinese culture is especially illuminating for those who want to make the idea of democracy more responsive to cultural variations. Dewey's intellectual effort to understand a foreign culture on its own terms was exemplary. If political leaders of the world could have the humility and sense of perspective that Dewey demonstrates, and if their citizens would appreciate knowing other cultures as enriching their own, the process of globalization in the twenty-first century would be more peaceful and rewarding for all.

I hope to open new dimensions for future research on Dewey and China. Studying the link between Dewey's later philosophy and his encounter with China may be worthwhile. One may examine Dewey's later works from the standpoint of his experiences in China and his encounter with Chinese intellectuals. My book focused on *The Public and Its Problems.* Dewey's other works, such as *Human Nature and Conduct* (1922), *Experience and Nature* (1925), or *Art as Experience* (1934), are also worth investigating. Apart from his social and political philosophy, other areas in Dewey's thinking, such as metaphysics, epistemology, or aesthetics, may also reflect the influence of this cross-cultural exchange.

On the other hand, one may reinvestigate Dewey's relationships with his Chinese disciples, such as Hu Shih, Tao Xingzhi, and Feng Youlan. Dewey's relationship with Hu was so complex that it deserves a study of its own. Previous studies often assumed that Hu was a legitimate spokesman for Deweyan pragmatism; I challenge this assumption and call for further research on the topic, which may yield important implications for contemporary studies in pragmatism. Dewey's relationship with Tao Xingzhi also presents an interesting case study. In my view, Tao's educational work in China represented a more authentic application of Dewey's educational theories, even though he claimed to have rejected Dewey when proposing his own theory of "teaching, learning and reflective acting."[1]

Moreover, scholarship has neglected Dewey's relationship with Feng Youlan, known for his scholarly work in Chinese philosophy.[2] Few knew that Feng was Dewey's student. Influenced by Dewey's huge reputation in China, Feng went to Columbia University to study philosophy in late 1919. Inspired by Dewey's comment that China could be understood only on its own terms, Feng conducted a philosophical inquiry into why

China had not developed science. In his essay, Feng contended that China lacked science because Chinese philosophers had always taught people to search for happiness within themselves, not in the outside world.[3] Feng's dissertation, which Dewey supervised and Feng completed in 1923, is particularly worth our attention because it may have contributed to Dewey's revived interest in metaphysics in the early 1920s. According to Westbrook, Dewey "surprisingly" returned to metaphysics in *Experience and Nature* (1925) after "badmouthing" it since the early 1890s.[4]

In his dissertation "A Comparative Study of Life Ideals," Feng examined the themes of man versus nature and of good versus evil in various philosophical schools of the East and the West.[5] Feng described the highest Confucian ideal as "not simply the realm of nature or the realm of human action, but a unity of both."[6] In *Experience and Nature*, Dewey argued for the unity of human experience and nature, contending that "experience is *of* and as well as *in* nature."[7] Even though Dewey's denunciation of dualism had been the benchmark of his thinking, it is reasonable to speculate that his exposure to Chinese philosophy through Feng may have helped explain his renewed interest in metaphysics.

Dewey's relationships with other Chinese intellectuals merit attention, such as that with Liang Shuming. As I mentioned in chapter three, Liang was a traditionalist who attempted to revive the enduring ideals in Confucianism while adapting them to meet China's need for modernization. Liang had read and valued Dewey's philosophy of education very highly. In his 1934 review of Dewey's *Democracy and Education*, Liang said, "[Dewey's theory of education] is marvelous. In his rendering, education encompasses everything because it connects the individual life with the social life."[8] According to Liang, Dewey's penetrating understanding about the vitality of life manifests in everything he said. Dewey embraced the dynamic, creative, autonomous, and progressive, while rejecting the passive, mechanical, and conservative. Liang criticized a life-negating tendency in mainstream Western scholarship and saw Dewey as a lonely fighter against this intellectual climate.[9] "If I have energy," Liang said, "I would like to fight by his side" to reaffirm life in Western philosophy.[10] In my opinion, Liang's insightful reading of Dewey suggests the meeting of two great minds that transcended the barrier of language and culture.

Remer remarked in 1920 that "Dewey cannot apply his own philosophy to Chinese life. It will require someone as close to Chinese thought as he is close to American thought to do this."[11] I believe that Liang Shuming was that person. He was one of the few people who understood Dewey's message—namely, that democracy for China had to come from within. Liang rejected both the Russian model of communism and the European model of democratic constitutionalism as appropriate for China because these models could, at best, be grafted onto Chinese society. Genuine democracy would evolve naturally out of the lived experiences of the people themselves.[12] The problem of China, Liang wrote, "is not a question of a revolutionary fight against whomever, but a question of internal cultural transformation as a basis for national salvation."[13] Liang devoted his life to promoting and implementing his idea of rural reconstruction, urging intellectuals to go to the countryside to mingle with the villagers to transform the culture at the grassroots level. Dewey made similar suggestions in his articles about China; examining the extent to which their views correspond would be interesting.

Finally, Dewey's reflections on the meaning of internationalism have rich implications for contemporary ethics of globalization, which involves issues such as the problem of cultural imperialism, the spread of democracy, the idea of national sovereignty, the authority of the United Nations, the distribution of foreign aid, and the justification for humanitarian intervention.[14] Apparently, these issues have become more urgent in our own time than in Dewey's. However, realizing that ethics should not stop at national boundaries is one thing, but determining what a global ethic should entail is another. This is a question that demands continuous thinking and rethinking. The lessons Dewey learned in China and the example he set before us are helpful in guiding our thoughts. Most important, we should attempt to understand one another's "philosophies of life" to avoid the clash of civilizations. We should all endeavor to create a genuine global community that is emotionally and intellectually sustained—that is truly of one world.

NOTES

❖

Chapter 1. Dewey and May Fourth China

1. According to Chow, the May Fourth movement covers the period roughly from 1917, as the new thoughts and new literature movements began to gain momentum, through 1921, when direct political control gradually replaced the appeal of intellectual reforms. Other historians have proposed to date the beginning of the movement in 1915—when feelings of national humiliation due to Japan's Twenty-One Demands began to shake intellectual circles—and the end in 1923 when the "science versus metaphysics" controversy subsided. Whichever time frame one adopts, one can claim that Dewey's visit to China, from May 1919 to July 1921, occurred in the midst of the movement. Tse-tsung Chow, *The May Fourth Movement: Intellectual Revolution in Modern China* (Stanford, CA: Stanford University Press, 1960), 5–6.

2. John S. Gregory, *The West and China since 1500* (New York: Palgrave MacMillan, 2003), 2.

3. Qtd. in Gregory, *The West and China,* 65.

4. Qtd. in Gregory, 74.

5. Qtd. in Gregory, 132.

6. Jonathan D. Spence, *The Search for Modern China* (New York: Norton, 1990), 231–35.

7. Gregory, 137.

8. References to Chinese names in the text will appear as surnames first. In the example of Hu Shih, Hu is the surname and Shih is the given name.

9. Jay Martin, *The Education of John Dewey: A Biography* (New York: Columbia University Press, 2002).

10. John Dewey to Dewey children, Tokyo, 13 March 1919, *The Correspondence of John Dewey* [CD-ROM], no. 03882 (Charlottesville, VA: InteLex, 2002). All subsequent letters by and to Dewey are cited from this collection and will be abbreviated as *Correspondence.*

11. John Dewey to Dewey children, Kyoto, 15 April 1919, *Correspondence,* no. 03889.

12. Martin, *The Education of John Dewey,* 304.

13. Qtd. in Martin, ibid.

14. John Dewey to Sabino Dewey, Kyoto, 22 April 1919, *Correspondence,* no. 03892.

15. John and Alice Chipman Dewey to Dewey children, Shanghai, 1 May 1919, *Correspondence,* no. 03898.

16. All references to Dewey's works are to *The Collected Works of John Dewey, 1882–1953: The Electronic Edition,* ed. Larry A. Hickman (Charlottesville, VA: InteLex, 1996). EW, MW, and LW are abbreviations for *The Early Works ,1881–1898* (5 volumes), *The Middle Works, 1899–1924* (15 volumes), and *The Later Works, 1925–1953* (17 volumes).

17. John Dewey to Dewey children, Beijing, 1 June 1919, *Correspondence,* no. 10759.

18. Clopton and Ou give a list of changes, which culminated in the 1922 education reform decree, to illustrate Dewey's influence: educational aims reconsidered, national school system modeled on the American 6-3-3 plan; child-centered education adopted; new pedagogy initiated; experimental schools multiplied; and student government encouraged. However high sounding these achievements may seem, further research is needed to examine if the top-down reform statues were ever widely translated into classroom practice. See Introduction to *Lectures in China, 1919–1920,* ed. and trans. Clopton Robert and Tsuin-chen Ou (Honolulu: University Press of Hawaii, 1973), 22–25.

19. Tsuin-chen Ou, "Dewey's Lectures and Influence in China," in *Guide to the Works of John Dewey,* ed. Ann Boydston (Carbondale: Southern Illinois University Press, 1970), 357.

20. Barry Keenan, *The Dewey Experiment in China: Educational Reform and Political Power in the Early Republic* (Cambridge, MA: Harvard University Press, 1977), 161.

21. Suzanne Pepper, *Radicalism and Education Reform in 20th Century China* (New York: Cambridge University Press, 1996), 60–62.

22. John Dewey to John Jacob Coss, Beijing, 13 January 1920, *Correspondence,* no. 04882.

23. Robert B. Westbrook, *John Dewey and American Democracy* (Ithaca, NY: Cornell University Press, 1991), 251.

24. Alan Ryan, *John Dewey and the High Tide of American Liberalism* (New York: Norton, 1995), 206.

25. Jane Dewey, "Biography of John Dewey," in *The Philosophy of John Dewey,* ed. Paul Arthur Schilpp (Chicago: Northwestern University Press, 1939), 42.

26. John Dewey to Nicholas Burray Butler, Shanghai, 3 May 1919, *Correspondence,* no. 04068.

27. Martin, 336.

28. Walter Lippmann to John Dewey, New York, 14 June 1921, *Correspondence,* no. 05208.

29. Ryan, *John Dewey and the High Tide of American Liberalism,* 223.

30. Chow, *The May Fourth Movement,* 327.

31. Youzhong Sun, "John Dewey in China: Yesterday and Today," *Transactions of the Charles S. Peirce Society* 35 (1999): 84.

32. For a noted example of this new scholarship, see Hongliang Gu (顧紅亮), *The Misreading of Pragmatism: The Influence of Dewey's Philosophy on Modern Chinese Philosophy* (實用主義的誤讀: 杜威哲學對中國現代哲學的影響) (Shanghai: East China Normal University Press, 2000). The book contains thoughtful discussions of the differences between Hu Shih and Dewey.

Chapter 2. Dewey as a Teacher

1. C. F. Remer, "John Dewey in China," *Millard's Review* 13 (3 July 1920): 267.

2. Yuanpei Cai (蔡元培), "A Speech Given at the Dinner Party of Dr. Dewey's Sixtieth Birthday" (在杜威博士60之生日晚餐會上之演說), in *Dewey on China* (杜威談中國), ed. Yihong Shen, 329–30.

3. Chongyi Feng (馮崇義), *Russell and China* (羅素與中國) (Beijing: Sanlian Bookstore, 1998), 108.

4. Caroline Moorehead, *Bertrand Russell: A Life* (New York: Viking, 1992), 342.

5. Qtd. in Chow, *The May Fourth Movement*, 59.

6. Keenan, *The Dewey Experiment*, 37.

7. *Lectures in China*, 127.

8. Ibid., 239.

9. Ibid., 167.

10. Dewey, "Democratic Developments in America" (美國之民治的發展), *Awakening* (覺悟), 21 June 1919, sec. 8. The translation is mine. *Awakening* is a major supplement of the Shanghai newspaper *Republic Daily* (民國日報).

11. These lectures were based partly on a class Dewey taught at Columbia University on moral and political philosophy from October 1915 to May 1916 (in which Hu Shih enrolled) and partly on the political commentaries Dewey wrote during the war years between 1917 and 1918. Two sets of class notes taken by Dewey's students at the seminar are available in *Research in the History of Economic Thought and Methodology: Lectures by John Dewey*, ed. Warren J. Samuels and Donald F. Koch (Greenwich, CT: Jai Press, 1989).

12. *Lectures in China*, 50.

13. Ibid., 62.

14. Ibid., 86.

15. Ibid., 71.

16. Ibid., 80.

17. Ibid., 118.

18. Ibid., 178.

19. Ibid., 154.

20. Ibid., 184.

21. Ibid., 298.

22. Ibid., 283.

23. Walter Feinberg, review of *Lectures in China, 1919–1920*, *Philosophy East and West* 25, no. 3 (1975): 366.

24. See Jiehua Li (黎潔華), "A List of Dewey's Activities in China" (杜威在華活動年表), in *Dewey on China*, ed. Yihong Shen, 391.

25. Hu, "Introductory Note by Hu Shih," in *Lectures in China*, 43–44.

26. John Dewey to John Jacob Coss, Nanjing, 22 April 1920, *Correspondence*, no. 04884.

27. Ralph Ross, Introduction to *The Middle Works of John Dewey: 1899–1924*, vol. 12, in MW 12: xxx.

28. Liang Qichao (梁啟超), one of the sponsors of Dewey's first-year visit in China, may have asked Dewey to introduce Bergson's thought. Liang visited

Bergson and Eucken in his trip to Europe during the war, hoping to obtain their advice on how to modernize China. However, he was told that the war manifested a bankruptcy of Western material civilization. After he returned, Liang proclaimed "the bankruptcy of science" and urged the youth to revere their spiritual tradition. See Chow, *The May Fourth Movement*, 328.

29. The summaries of Dewey's individual lectures Clopton and Ou provided were very helpful. See the appendix in *Lectures in China*.

30. John Dewey to Dewey children, Beijing, 1 April 1920, *Correspondence*, no. 03593. In the original texts of Dewey's letters, apostrophes were often left out, as in "cant." When quoting Dewey's letters, I will use brackets to indicate my modifications, as in "[can't]."

31. Dewey, "Present Opportunities for the Teaching Profession" (教師職業之現在機會), *Morning Post* (晨報), 24 June 1921, sec. 7.

32. John Dewey to Albert C. Barnes, Beijing, 5 December 1920, *Correspondence*, no. 04113.

33. Ibid.

34. *Lectures in China*, 319.

35. Ibid., 321–22.

36. Yihong Shen (沈益洪), Introduction to *Russell on China* (羅素談中國), ed. Yihong Shen (Hangzhou: Zhejiang Literature and Art, 2001), 4.

37. Feng, *Russell and China*, 140.

38. Russell to Colette O'Niel, Beijing, 6 January 1921, *The Selected Letters of Bertrand Russell: the Public Years, 1914–1970*, ed. Nicholas Griffin (London: Routledge, 2001), 217.

39. Qtd. in Moorehead, *Bertrand Russell*, 326.

40. Russell to Elizabeth Russell, Beijing, 16 February 1921, *The Selected Letters*, 224.

41. Dora Black wrote in a letter that "everywhere we are treated like an Emperor and Empress." See Moorehead, *Bertrand Russell*, 323.

42. Russell to Colette O'Neil, Beijing, 21 February 1921, qtd. in Chongyi Feng, *Russell and China*, 112.

43. Russell, "The Bolsheviks and World Politics" (布爾什維克與世界政治), in *Russell on China*, ed. Yihong Shen, 309, 314.

44. John Dewey to Albert C. Barnes, Beijing, 5 December 1920, *Correspondence*, no, 04113.

45. Duxiu Chen, "A Letter to Mr. Russell from Duxiu" (獨秀致羅素先生的信), in *Russell on China*, 379.

46. Russell, "Bolshevik Thoughts" (布爾什維克的思想), in *Russell on China*, 320.

47. Russell, "China's Road to Freedom" (中國到自由之路), in *Russell on China*, 327.

48. John Dewey to Dewey children, Changsha, 26 October 1920, *Correspondence*, no. 03946.

49. Russell to H. C. Emery, Beijing, 14 January 1921, *The Selected Letters*, 219.

50. John Dewey to Albert C. Barnes, Beijing, 5 December 1920, *Correspondence*, no. 04113.

51. Bertrand Russell, *The Problem of China* (London: Allen and Unwin, 1922), 185.

52. Remer, "John Dewey in China," 268.

53. "Report from the Farewell Banquet for Dewey" (五團體恭踐杜威之言論), *Morning Post*, 26 May 1921, sec. 3. The translation is mine.

54. John Dewey to Albert C. Barnes, Beijing, 5 December 1920, *Correspondence*, no. 04113.

55. Yu-sheng Lin, *The Crisis of Chinese Consciousness: Radical Antitraditionalism in the May Fourth Era* (Madison: University of Wisconsin Press, 1979), 27.

56. Clopton and Ou, Translators' Note, *Lectures in China*, 34. In their translation of Dewey's lectures into English, Clopton and Ou may have attempted to reduce potential discrepancies and to recover what Dewey might have actually said. For the purpose of recovery, these translations are laudable and important. However, for the purpose of understanding Dewey's reception in China, one needs to read the Chinese texts.

57. Jim E. Tiles, "Democracy as Culture," in *Justice and Democracy: Cross-Cultural Perspectives*, ed. Ron Bontekoe and Marietta Stepaniants (Honolulu: University of Hawaii Press, 1997), 125.

58. Dewey, "Democratic Developments in America." In this section of the chapter, the translation of Chinese materials into English is mine unless otherwise stated.

59. See Westbrook, *John Dewey and American Democracy*, 167.

60. John Dewey to Dewey children, Beijing, 5 June 1919, *Correspondence*, no. 10761.

61. Jerome Grieder, *Hu Shih and the Chinese Renaissance* (Cambridge, MA: Harvard University Press, 1970), 45.

62. Xiping (希平), "My Response to Dewey's Experimentalism" (我對杜威試驗主義的感想), *Awakening*, 27 July 1920, Commentary section.

63. John Dewey to Dewey children, Shanghai, 13 May 1919, *Correspondence*, no. 10755.

64. Chow, 230.

65. *John Dewey's Five Major Lecture Series* (杜威五大講演) (Hefai: Anhui Education Press, 1999), 114.

66. Lin, *The Crisis of Chinese Consciousness*, 99.

67. Scholars have disagreed as to what Hu truly meant by his proclamation of "total Westernization" (全盤西化). Grieder thinks that Hu intended "to discredit the kind of dogged intellectual reaction," not to annihilate "every vestige of traditional Chinese culture." Lin holds that Hu urged to the Chinese to accept "the modern civilization of the West to the greatest possible extent." See Grieder, *Hu Shih and the Chinese Renaissance*, 287, and Lin, 83.

68. Guangdi Mei (梅光迪), *Writings of Professor K. T. Mei* (梅光迪文錄) (Taipei: Chinese Library, 1968), 5–9.

69. Chow, 282.

70. *John Dewey's Five Major Lecture Series*, 6, emphasis added. In the Clopton and Ou's English translation, the same passage reads: "The common weakness

of extreme radicalism and extreme conservatism as I have described them is their dependence on sweeping generalizations." *Lectures in China*, 53.

71. Hu, "More Talk of Problems and Less Talk of Isms" (多談些問題少談些主義), in *Dewey and China* (杜威與中國), ed. Baogui Zhang (Shijiazhuang: Hebei People's Press, 2001), 186.

72. Dazhao Li (李大釗), "Again on Problems versus Isms" (再論問題與主義), in *Dewey and China*, ed. Baogui Zhang, 188.

73. Maurice Meisner, *Li Ta-Chao and the Origin of Chinese Marxism* (Cambridge, MA: Harvard University Press, 1967), 106.

74. Grieder, 49.

75. Meisner, 108.

76. Alice Chipman Dewey to Dewey children and Sabino Dewey, Beijing, 1 June 1919, *Correspondence*, no. 03907.

77. John Dewey to Wendell T. Bush, Beijing, 1 August 1919, *Correspondence*, no. 05019.

78. Nancy F. Sizer, "John Dewey's Ideas in China, 1919–21," *Comparative Education Review* 10 (1966): 401.

79. Meisner, 107–8.

80. Keenan, 123–24.

81. Ibid., 161.

82. In my opinion, Hu Shih often parroted Dewey. Hu's award-winning essay from the American Association for International Conciliation in 1916 was an application of Dewey's concept of force. In his essay Hu claimed, "the real problem [with the world] is to seek a more economical and therefore more sufficient way of employing force; a substitute for the present crude form and wasteful use of force." Qtd. in Grieder, 60.

83. Lin, 93.

84. Sor-hoon Tan, "China's Pragmatist Experiment in Democracy: Hu Shih's Pragmatism and Dewey's Influence in China," in *The Range of Pragmatism and the Limits of Philosophy*, ed. Richard Shusterman (Oxford: Blackwell, 2005), 56.

85. Grieder, 121.

86. Lin, 28.

87. Ibid., 86.

88. Vera Schwarcz, *The Chinese Enlightenment: Intellectuals and the Legacy of the May Fourth Movement of 1919* (Berkeley: University of California Press, 1986), 38.

89. Hu, "The Meaning of New Thought Tide" (新思潮的意義), in *A Collection of Hu Shih's Educational Writings* (胡適教育論著選), ed. Jian Bai and Yanyun Liu (Beijing: People's Education Press, 1994), 108.

90. Shih Hu, "John Dewey in China," in *Philosophy and Culture—East and West*, ed. Charles Am Moore (Honolulu: University of Hawaii Press, 1962), 768.

91. Ibid.

92. Tan, "China's Pragmatist Experiment," 60.

93. Ibid., Sor-hoon Tan speculates that Hu Shih "was an important pragmatist" and that his attempt to "pragmatism as a philosophical method to

solve human problems in China has something to teach us." For a different perspective, see Hongliang Gu, *The Misreading of Pragmatism.*

94. Hu's translations of Dewey's lectures—especially where Dewey commented on the student movement—may have misguided Tan to speculate that Dewey shared Hu Shih's rather negative judgment about the students' political activism. Tan, "China's Pragmatist Experiment," 55.

95. Ibid., 58.

96. John Dewey to John Jacob Coss, 13 January 1920, *Correspondence*, no. 04882.

97. John Dewey to Dewey children, Beijing, 1 April 1920, *Correspondence*, no. 03593.

98. Remer, "John Dewey in China," 267.

99. Ibid.

100. Clopton and Ou, Introduction to *Lectures in China*, 25.

101. Jane Cauvel, "Dewey's Message to China," in *Hypatia : Essays in Classics, Comparative Literature, and Philosophy*, ed. William M. Calder III, Ulrich K. Goldsmith, and Phyllis B. Kenevan (Boulder: Colorado Associated University Press, 1985), 228.

Chapter 3. The Reception of Dewey in China

1. Dewey once noted in his letter that many in his audience "don't really understand" his lectures on "Types of Thinking." He estimated attendance would gradually drop in subsequent meetings. John Dewey to Wendell T. Bush, Beijing, 13 November 1919, *Correspondence*, no. 05022.

2. Keenan, *The Dewey Experiment*, 34.

3. Jin Zhu朱進, "Why Are Scholars Revered by the World?" (學者何以為世人所崇拜), *New Education* (新教育) 1 (1919): 361.

4. Kui (魁), "Experimentalism and Scientific Life" (實驗主義與科學的生活), *Academic Lamp*, 15 November 1919.

5. Qtd. in John Hersey, *The Call* (New York: Knopf, 1985), 334.

6. Zhixi (志希), "Dr. Dewey's *School and Society*" (杜威博士的學校與社會), *Renaissance* (新潮) 2 (1919): 187. Zhixi is the pen name of Lo Jialun (羅家倫).

7. Zhixi, "Dr. Dewey's 'Moral Principles in Education'" (杜威博士的德育原理), *Renaissance* 2 (1919): 192.

8. Qianzhi Zhu (朱謙之), "A Manifesto against Examinations" (反抗考試的宣言), *Beijing University Student Weekly* (北京大學學生週刊), 13 (28 March 1920).

9. Jiehua Li, "A List of Dewey's Activities in China," 396.

10. Ibid., 377.

11. John Dewey to Dewey family, Nanjing, 11 April 1920, *Correspondence*, no. 03916.

12. Boan (柏盦), "The Responses to Dewey from the Educational Circle of Hangzhou" (杭州教育界對杜威的感想), *Academic Lamp*, 23 June 1920.

13. T. D., "A Critique of Dewey's Lecture" (評杜威底演講), *Awakening*, 18 June 1920, Random Thoughts section.

14. Xiping (希平), "My Response to Dewey's Experimentalism" (我對杜威試驗主義的感想), *Awakening*, 27 July 1920, Commentary section.

15. John Dewey to Albert C. Barnes, Peitaho, 12 September 1920, *Correspondence*, no. 04102.

16. John Dewey to Albert C. Barnes, Beijing, 5 December 1920, *Correspondence*, no. 04113.

17. Benjamin I. Schwartz, *Chinese Communism and the Rise of Mao* (Cambridge, MA: Harvard University Press, 1951), 25.

18. John Dewey to Albert C. Barnes, Beijing, 12 September 1920, *Correspondence*, no. 04102.

19. Zhenying (震瀛), "My Hope for Bertrand Russell" (我對羅素的希望), *Awakening*, 15 October 1920, Commentary section.

20. Fulu (伏廬), "Dr. Dewey Is Gone Today" (杜威博士今日去了), *Morning Post*, 11 July 1921, Miscellaneous Notes section. Fulu is the pen name of Sun Fuyuan (孫伏園). Sun also wrote an essay on the same day to commemorate Bertrand Russell, but he said that Russell's influence on the Chinese was not comparable to that of Dewey. See Fulu, "Mr. Russell Is also Gone Today" (羅素先生今日也去了), *Morning Post*, 11 July 1921, Miscellaneous Notes section.

21. Arif Dirlik, *The Origins of Chinese Communism* (New York: Oxford University Press), 71.

22. Chow, *The May Fourth Movement*, 248.

23. Ibid., 213.

24. Grieder, *Hu Shih and the Chinese Renaissance*, 184.

25. Schwartz, *Chinese Communism and the Rise of Mao*, 19.

26. Duxiu Chen (陳獨秀), "The Basis for the Realization of Democracy" (實行民治的基礎), in *Selected Writings of Chen Duxiu* (陳獨秀著作選), ed. Jianshu Ren, Tongmo Chang, and Xinzhong Wu, vol. 2 (Shanghai: Shanghai People's Press, 1993), 29.

27. Ibid., 29–30.

28. Chow, *The May Fourth Movement*, 231.

29. John Dewey to Dewey children, Beijing, 10 June 1919, *Correspondence*, no. 03910.

30. Chen, "The Basis for the Realization of Democracy," 31

31. Chow, 232.

32. Chen, "The Basis for the Realization of Democracy," 32.

33. Ibid., 35.

34. Qtd. in Schwartz, 22.

35. Dirlik, *The Origins of Chinese Communism*, 53–54.

36. Schwartz, 23.

37. Ibid., 21–22.

38. Chow, 232.

39. Dirlik, 64.

40. John Dewey to Walter S. Drysdale, Beijing, 1 December 1920, *Correspondence*, no. 06412.

41. John Dewey to Albert C. Barnes, Beijing, 5 December 1920, *Correspondence*, no. 04113.

42. Juetian Fei (費覺天), "A Critique of Dewey's Social and Political Philosophy" (評杜威底社會與政治哲學), *The Review of Reviews* (評論之評論), 2 (1921): 4.

43. John Dewey to Albert C. Barnes, Beitaiho, 12 September 1920, *Correspondence*, no. 04102.

44. Qiubai Qu (瞿秋白), "Pragmatism and Revolutionary Philosophy" (實驗主義與革命哲學), in *Selected Writings of Qu Qiubai* (瞿秋白選集) (Beijing: People's Press, 1985), 145.

45. Ibid., 147.

46. Ibid., 151.

47. Susanne K. Langer, qtd. in Lin, *The Crisis of Chinese Consciousness*, 57.

48. Qichao Liang (梁啟超), "Travel Impressions from Europe" (歐遊心影錄), in *A Selection of Essays on the Controversy over Eastern and Western Civilizations before and after May Fourth* (五四前後東西文化問題論戰文選), ed. Song Chen (Beijing: Xinhua, 1989), 349–90.

49. Shuming Liang (梁漱溟), *Eastern and Western Cultures and Their Philosophies* (東西文化及其哲學) (Taipei: Commercial Press, 2002), 2.

50. Chow, 282.

51. Fenglin Mo (繆鳳林), "A Review of Dewey's *Democracy and Education*" (評杜威平民與教育), *The Critical Review* (學衡)10 (1922): 5–6.

52. Jiangling Wu (吳江玲), "A Critique of Dewey's Philosophy of Education" (評杜威之教育哲學), *Academic Lamp*, 22 October 1922.

53. Zhaoyin Lin (林昭音), "A Few Questions about Dewey's *Democracy and Education*" (讀杜威平民主義與教育之幾個疑問), *The Chinese Educational Circles* (中華教育界) 12 (1923): 1–6.

54. Ibid., 5.

55. Following Dewey and Russell, Tagore was invited to visit China in 1924.

56. Juemin Gao (高覺敏), "The Problems of Americanized Education" (囫圇吞棗式的美國化教育), *Journal of Education* (教育雜誌) 17 (1925): 3.

57. Mouzu Wang (汪懋祖), "The Problems of Education at the Present Time and Their Remedies" (現時我國教育上之弊病與其救治方略), *Critical Review* 22 (1923): 1.

58. The American educator Paul Monroe (1869–1949) was a colleague of Dewey at Columbia University and was invited to China in September 1921 to help reform Chinese education.

59. Shaohan He (何紹韓), "The So-Called New Education" (余之所謂新教育), *Educational Tide* (教育潮), 1 (1919): 51–52.

60. Shoying (瘦影), "The Real Meaning of Pragmatism Is Not 'Coping-with-the-Environment-Ism'" (實驗主義的真義絕不是對付環境主義), *Beijing University Student Weekly* 13 (28 March 1920).

61. Hu, "Fundamental Ideas in Dewey's Philosophy" (杜威哲學的根本概念), in *Dewey and China*, ed. Baoqui Zhang, 162–65.

62. Duxiu Chen, "What Is New Education?" (新教育是什麼), in *A Collection of Educational Essays by Chen Duxiu* (陳獨秀教育論著選), ed. Xiemei Qi and Zhude Shao (Beijing: People's Education Press, 1995), 281–90.

63. Even though he discarded Dewey's political ideas in favor of Marxism, Chen incorporated many of Dewey's educational ideas into his own thinking

about education reform. For instance, Chen took Dewey's idea that schools should reflect local cultures and suggested that Guandong should establish "Silk schools" because the area was noted for its silk production, and that Northern provinces should establish "Forest schools" to contribute to their local log industry. Ibid., 286.

64. Haifeng Liu (劉海峰), *Educational Angles of Civil Service Examinations* (科舉考試的教育視角) (Wuhan: Hubei Education Press, 1995), 215.

65. Ibid., 209.

66. Harold W. Stevenson and James W. Stigler, *The Learning Gap: Why Our Schools Are Failing and What We Can Learn from Japanese and Chinese Education* (New York: Simon and Schuster, 1992).

67. Randolph S. Bourne, "Twilight of Idols," in *War and the Intellectuals: Essays by Randolph S. Bourne*, ed. Carl Resek (New York: Harper Torchbooks, 1964), 60–61.

68. Qtd. in Westbrook, *John Dewey and American Democracy*, 383.

69. Ibid., 386–87.

70. The translated essay, "New Culture in China"(中國新文化), was published in the *Morning Post*, 28–31 June, 1921.

71. "The Chinese Philosophy of Life" (中國人的人生哲學) was translated by Yuzhi (愉之) and published in *The Eastern Miscellany* (東方雜誌) 19 (1923): 21–32. A later title for the article was "As the Chinese Think."

Chapter 4. Dewey as a Learner

1. Keenan, *The Dewey Experiment*, 25. Keenan's judgment is based on an article Dewey wrote about the New Culture movement in China in which Dewey modestly acknowledged an intellectual debt to "a Chinese friend" for explaining to him different stages of foreign influence on China. Those who were conversant with Dewey's style would know that Dewey sometimes could be overly modest.

2. John Dewey to Dewey children, Beijing, 1 June 1919, *Correspondence*, no. 10759.

3. John Dewey to Dewey children, Beijing, 20 June 1919, *Correspondence*, no. 10764.

4. See Westbrook, *John Dewey and American Democracy*, 86.

5. Ibid., 84.

6. Ibid., 88, 87.

7. Ibid., 88.

8. Dewey once compared Hu to another Chinese intellectual he met, saying that this man was "more practical than our usual guide and philosopher [meaning Hu]." John Dewey to Dewey children, 9 November 1919, Beijing, *Correspondence*, no. 03572.

9. In a letter on 2 June, 1919, either Alice or Dewey told their children: "Meanwhile, we wondered around, planned on how it [a particular object] could be made into use when revolution comes. Get rid of the idea that China

has had a revolution and is a republic. That point is just where we have been deceived in the United States." Alice Chipman Dewey (or John Dewey?) to Dewey children, Beijing, 2 June 1919, *Correspondence*, no. 10760.

10. John Dewey to Walter S. Drysdale, Beijing, 1 December 1920, *Correspondence*, no. 06412.

11. Alice Chipman Dewey to Dewey family, 13 June 1920, Hangzhou, *Correspondence*, no. 03937.

12. In his canonical work, *The May Fourth Movement*, Chow Tse-tsung drew substantially from Dewey's insightful comments about May Fourth China.

13. See Ryan, *John Dewey and High Tide of American Liberalism*, 204.

14. John Dewey to Albert C. Barnes, Beijing, 15 September 1919, *Correspondence*, no. 04103.

15. John Dewey to Herbert W. Schneider, Beijing, 3 January 1921, *Correspondence*, no. 03491.

16. John Dewey to Albert C. Barnes, Beijing, 15 September 1919, *Correspondence*, no. 04103.

17. John Dewey to Dewey children, Beijing, 1 June 1919, *Correspondence*, no. 10759.

18. Michael Eldridge, *Transforming Experience: John Dewey's Cultural Instrumentalism* (Nashville, TN: Vanderbilt University Press, 1998), 14.

19. Alice Chipman Dewey to Frederick A. Dewey, Beijing, 15 February 1920, *Correspondence*, no. 03585.

20. John Dewey to Dewey children, Beijing, 9 November 1919, *Correspondence*, no. 03572.

21. John Dewey to John Jacob Coss, Beijing, 13 January 1920, *Correspondence*, no. 04882.

22. John Dewey to Albert C. Barnes, Beijing, 15 October, 1920, *Correspondence*, no. 04106.

23. Albert C. Barnes to John Dewey, Philadelphia, 4 January 1921, *Correspondence*, no. 04116.

24. John Dewey to Albert C. Barnes, Beijing, 13 March 1921, *Correspondence*, no. 04120.

25. Feng, *Russell and China*, 214.

26. Bertrand Russell to Clifford Allen, Beijing, 13 December 1920, *The Selected Letters*, 213.

27. Bertrand Russell to Colette O'Neil, Beijing, 6 January 1921, *The Selected Letters*, 216. Russell proposed the plan for his book to a publisher immediately after he returned to England because he needed the money to support his newborn child. Clark Ronald, *The Life of Bertrand Russell* (New York: Knopf, 1976).

28. John Macrae to John Dewey, New York, 28 October 1919, *Correspondence*, no. 04704. A short collection of Dewey's essays related to the Washington Conference was published in 1921, with the title, *China, Japan and the U. S. A.* (New York: Republic Publishing, 1921).

29. Walter Lippmann to John Dewey, Wading, 16 June 1921, *Correspondence*, no. 05208.

30. Russell said that the distinctive merit of Western civilization is the scientific method, whereas the distinctive merit of the Chinese is "a just conception of the ends of life." Bertrand Russell, *The Problem of China*, 205.

31. C. F. Remer, "John Dewey's Responsibility for American Opinion," *Millard's Review* 13 (10 July 1920): 321–22.

32. In 1946 when Dewey received the invitation to lecture in China, he decided to accept it, even though his family was concerned for his safety and health. However, the invitation was cancelled due to unsettling political situations. Jay Martin, *The Education of John Dewey*, 326–27.

33. Jane Dewey, "Biography of John Dewey," in *The Philosophy of John Dewey*, ed. Paul Arthur Schillipp (Chicago: Northwestern University Press, 1939), 42.

34. Jonathan Spence, *To Change China: Western Advisors in China, 1620–1960* (New York: Penguin Books, 1980), 290–92.

35. Qtd. in Martin, 318.

36. Steven C. Rockefeller, *John Dewey: Religious Faith and Democratic Humanism* (New York: Columbia University Press, 1991), 312.

37. John Dewey to John Jacob Coss, Beijing, 1 April 1920, *Correspondence*, no. 04884.

38. John Dewey to James H. Tufts, Beijing, 23 February 1921, *Correspondence*, no. 07207.

39. These selected letters were published in 1920 under the title, *Letters from China and Japan*.

40. Reviewed in *Boston Evening Transcript*, 1 June 1920; in *New York Tribune*, 16 May 1920; in *Pacific Review*, December 1920, 429–30, by J. E. P. However, two reviews were critical. One criticized Dewey's literary utterances and paucity of expression, which Otto Keller reviewed in *St. Louis Post-Dispatch*, 7 August 1920. Another reviewer faulted the Deweys for misspelling Japanese words, saying that one ought to feel "astonished that our travelers ever undertook their journey to the Orient, with their complete ignorance of it, its soul, its history, its problems. It is never too late to learn and the Orient needs first-hand study," as reviewed in *Unity*, 4 November 1920. The accusation here is not quite fair, at least, to Mrs. Dewey, who actually started to read up on Japanese civilization and art when the plan for their trip was finalized. See Martin, *The Education of John Dewey*, 310. Generally, Dewey's impressions of Japan were thought to be less penetrating than those of China.

41. John Jacob Coss to John Dewey, New York, 11 January 1921, *Correspondence*, no. 04889. According to the Center for Dewey Studies, no record shows that Dewey had actually taught such a class.

42. Martin, 336.

43. David Sidorsky, Introduction to *The Later Works of John Dewey: 1925–1953*, vol. 3, in LW 3: xxxi.

44. Qtd. in Martin, 340.

45. John Dewey to John Jacob Coss, Beijing, 13 January 1920, *Correspondence*, no. 04882.

46. Martin, 364.

47. Ibid., 327.

Chapter 5. The Influence of China on Dewey's Social and Political Philosophy

1. Donald F. Koch, "Internal Conflict and the Development of Dewey's Moral, Political and Legal Philosophy," in *Research in the History of Economic Thought and Methodology,* ed. Warren J. Samuels and Donald F. Koch (Greenwich, CT: Jai Press, 1989), 36.

2. Gary Bullert, *The Politics of John Dewey* (New York: Prometheus Books, 1983), 39.

3. John Dewey to James H. Tufts, Beijing, 23 February 1921, *Correspondence,* no. 07207.

4. John Dewey to Dewey children, Shanghai, 13 May 1919, *Correspondence,* no. 10754.

5. Ibid.

6. Peter Manicas, "John Dewey: Anarchism and the Political State," qtd. in Sor-hoon Tan, *Confucian Democracy: A Deweyan Reconstruction* (Albany: State University of New York Press, 2003), 124.

7. Jonathan G. Utley, "American Views of China, 1900–1915," in *America Views China: American Images of China Then and Now,* ed. Jonathan Goldstein, Jerry Israel, and Hilary Conroy (Bethlehem, PA: Lehigh University Press, 1991).

8. Stephen C. Pepper, review of *The Public and Its Problems, The International Journal of Ethics* 38 (1928): 478.

9. Jim E. Tiles, "Democracy as Culture," in *Justice and Democracy: Cross-Cultural Perspectives,* ed. Ron Bontekoe and Marietta Stepaniants (Honolulu: University of Hawaii Press, 1997), 121.

10. Westbrook, *John Dewey and American Democracy,* 319.

11. Tan, *Confucian Democracy,* 284.

12. Samuel P. Huntington, "Democracy's Third Wave," *Journal of Democracy* 2 (1991), 24.

13. Wei-ming Tu, *Confucian Ethics Today: The Singapore Challenge* (Singapore: Curriculum Development Institute of Singapore), 90.

14. David L. Hall and Roger T. Ames, *The Democracy of the Dead: Dewey, Confucius, and the Hope for Democracy in China* (Chicago: Open Court, 1999), 7.

15. Steven J. Hood, "The Myth of Asian-Style Democracy," *Asian Survey* 38 (1998): 853–66.

16. Edward Friedman, "Does China Have the Cultural Preconditions for Democracy?" *Philosophy East and West* 49 (1999), 354.

17. Hall and Ames, *The Democracy of the Dead,* 11.

18. Ibid., 176.

19. Tan, 572.

20. Hall and Ames, 216–17.

21. Ibid., 173.

22. Ibid.

23. Ibid., 205.

24. Hall and Ames, 160.

25. Tan, 587.

26. Hall and Ames, 184.

27. Qtd. in Russell Fox, "Confucian and Communitarian Response to Liberal Democracy," *The Review of Politics* 59 (1997), 579.

28. Hall and Ames, 160.

29. Russell Fox, 582.

30. Ibid., 584.

31. Hall and Ames, 158.

32. Tan, 100.

33. Ibid., 104.

34. Hall and Ames, 165.

35. Ibid., 166.

Chapter 6. Continuing the Dialogue on Dewey and China

1. Tao transformed Dewey's "education as life" to "life as education," his "school as society" to "society as school," and his "learning by doing" to "teaching, learning and reflective doing." Zhixin Su, "Teaching, Learning and Reflective Acting: A Dewey Experiment in Chinese Teacher Education," *Teachers College Record* 98 (1996).

2. Feng was the author of *A History of Chinese Philosophy*, trans. Derk Bodde (Princeton, NJ: Princeton University Press, 1952).

3. Youlan Feng, "Why China Has No Science: An Interpretation of the History and Consequences of Chinese Philosophy," *International Journal of Ethics* 32 (1922). Feng opened his essay by acknowledging Dewey's insights about China. Interestingly, Feng's essay appeared around the same time as Dewey's "As the Chinese Think." A receptive reader may wonder whether Dewey's essay had any similarities with that of Feng. To answer the question, I studied Feng's essay and checked his book on the history of Chinese philosophy, I found that Dewey's interpretation of the Taoist concept of nonaction as "an act of moral doing" was uniquely his own.

4. Westbrook, 321.

5. Youlan Feng, *The Hall of Three Pines*, trans. Denis C. Maire (Honolulu: University of Hawaii Press, 2000), 214–15.

6. Ibid., 212.

7. Qtd. in Westbrook, 322.

8. Shuming Liang, "Fundamental Ideas in Dewey's Philosophy of Education" (杜威教育哲學之根本概念), in *A Collection of Educational Essays by Liang Shuming* (梁漱溟教育論著選), ed. Qiufan Ma (Beijing: People's Education Press, 1994), 120.

9. The mainstream Western intellectual orientation to which Liang referred probably was the postwar crisis of meaning.

10. Ibid., 122.

11. Remer, "John Dewey in China," 267.

12. Democratic liberalism, as Liang understood it, was not in keeping with the spirit of the Chinese people because it required each citizen to assert his or her individual liberties. Chinese social life was characterized by contentedness

and forbearance, which Liang considered to be unique virtues. The Chinese would not assert or fight for individual liberties as Europeans do because the Chinese lacked a solid concept of the individual self. Shuming Liang, *A Final Reflection on the National Salvation Movement in China* (中國民族自救運動之最後覺悟) (Taipei: Academic Press, 1971), 117–22.

13. Ibid., 184.

14. Peter Singer, *One World: The Ethics of Globalization* (New Haven, CT: Yale University Press, 2002).

BIBLIOGRAPHY

Books and Essays by John Dewey Referred to in the Text

In order of appearance in *The Collected Works of John Dewey, 1882–1953: The Electronic Edition.* Edited by Larry A. Hickman. Charlottesville, VA: InteLex, 1996. Early Works, Middle Works, and Later Woks refer to *The Early Works, 1881–1898* (5 volumes), *The Middle Works, 1899–1924* (15 volumes), and *The Later Works, 1925–1953* (17 volumes).

Books

German Philosophy and Politics. In *Middle Works* 8: 135–204.
Democracy and Education. In *Middle Works* 9.
Reconstruction in Philosophy. In *Middle Works* 12: 79–201.
The Public and Its Problems. In *Later Works* 2: 235–381
Ethics . In *Later Works* 7.
Art as Experience. In *Later Works* 10.
Liberalism and Social Action. In *Later Works* 11: 3–65.
Freedom and Culture. In *Later Works* 13: 65–188.
Lectures in China, 1919–1920. Edited and translated by Robert W. Clopton and Tsuin-chen Ou. Honolulu: University of Hawaii Press, 1973.

Essays

"The Ethics of Democracy." In *Early Works* 1: 228–50.
"Interest in Relation to the Training of the Will." In *Early Works* 5: 113–46.
"Progress?" In *Middle Works* 10: 234–43.
"Conscience and Compulsion." In *Middle Works* 10: 260–65.
"On the Two Sides of the Eastern Sea." In *Middle Works* 11: 174–79.
"The Discrediting of Idealism." In *Middle Works* 11: 180–85.
"The Student Revolt in China." In *Middle Works* 11: 186–91.
"The International Duel in China." In *Middle Works* 11: 192–98.
"Transforming the Mind of China." In *Middle Works* 11: 205–14.
"Chinese National Sentiment." In *Middle Works* 11: 215–27.
"The American Opportunity in China." In *Middle Works* 11: 228–34.
"Our Share in Drugging China." In *Middle Works* 11: 235–40.
"Our National Dilemma." In *Middle Works* 12: 3–7.
"How Reaction Helps." In *Middle Works* 12: 17–21.
"The Sequel of the Student Revolt." In *Middle Works* 12: 22–27.

"Shantung, as Seen from Within." In *Middle Works* 12: 28–40.
"The New Leaven in Chinese Politics." In *Middle Works* 12: 41–50.
"What Holds China Back?" In *Middle Works* 12: 51–59.
"Is China a Nation?" In *Middle Works* 13: 72–78.
"The Far Eastern Deadlock." In *Middle Works* 13: 79–85.
"Old China and New." In *Middle Works* 13: 93–107.
"New Culture in China." In *Middle Works* 13: 108–20.
"The Issues at Washington." In *Middle Works* 13: 173–90.
"America and Chinese Education." In *Middle Works* 13: 228–32.
"Federalism in China." In *Middle Works* 13: 149–55.
"A Parting of the Ways for America." In *Middle Works* 13: 159–90.
"As the Chinese Think." In *Middle Works* 13: 215–27.
"Divided China." In *Middle Works* 13: 127–38.
"The Tenth Anniversary of the Republic of China." In *Middle Works* 13: 147–48.
"China and the West." In *Middle Works* 15: 215–18.
"We Should Deal with China as a Nation to Nation." In *Middle Works* 15: 185–88.
"America and the Far East." In *Later Works* 2: 173–75.
"Creative Democracy—The Task before Us." In *Later Works* 14: 225–52.

Letters Written by and to Dewey Quoted in the Text

The Correspondence of John Dewey [CD-ROM]. Edited by Larry A. Hickman. Charlottesville, VA: InteLex, 2002.

Printed Lectures and Books by Dewey in Chinese

John Dewey's Five Major Lecture Series (杜威五大講演). Translated by Hu Shih (胡適). Hefai: Anhui Education Press, 1999.
"Present Opportunities for the Teaching Profession" (教師職業之現在機會). *Morning Post* (晨報), 24 June 1921, sec. 7.
"Democratic Developments in America" (美國之民治的發展). *Awakening* (覺悟), 21 June 1919, sec. 8.
"New Culture in China" (中國新文化). *Morning Post* (晨報), 28–31 June 1921.
"Chinese Philosophy of Life" (中國人的人生哲學). Translated by Yuzhi (愉之). *The Eastern Miscellany* (東方雜誌) 19 (1923): 21–32.

Secondary Sources in English

Bourne, Randolph S. "Twilight of Idols." In *War and the Intellectuals: Essays by Randolph S. Bourne,* edited by Carl Resek, 53–64. New York: Harper Torchbooks, 1964.
Bullert, Gary. *The Politics of John Dewey.* New York: Prometheus Books, 1983.
Cauvel, Jane. "Dewey's Message to China." In *Hypatia: Essays in Classics, Comparative Literature, and Philosophy,* edited by William M. Calder III, Ulrich K. Goldsmith, and Phyllis B. Kenevan, 227–39. Boulder: Colorado Associated University Press, 1985.

Chow, Tse-tsung. *The May Fourth Movement: Intellectual Revolution in Modern China.* Stanford, CA: Stanford University Press, 1960.

Clopton, Robert W. and Tsuin-chen Ou. Introduction to *John Dewey: Lectures in China, 1919–1920.* Honolulu: University of Hawaii Press, 1973.

Dewey, Jane. "Biography of John Dewey." In *The Philosophy of John Dewey,* edited by Paul Arthur Schilpp, 3–45. Chicago: Northwestern University Press, 1939.

Dirlik, Arif. *The Origins of Chinese Communism.* New York: Oxford University Press, 1989.

Eldridge, Michael. *Transforming Experience: John Dewey's Cultural Instrumentalism.* Nashville, TN: Vanderbilt University Press, 1998.

Feinberg, Walter. Review of *John Dewey: Lectures in China, 1919–20. Philosophy East and West* 25 (1975): 365–69.

Feng, Youlan. *The Hall of Three Pines.* Translated by Denis C. Mair. Honolulu: University of Hawaii Press, 2000.

———. "Why China Has No Science: An Interpretation of the History and Consequences of Chinese Philosophy." *International Journal of Ethics* 32 (1922): 237–63.

Fox, Russell Arben. "Confucian and Communitarian Responses to Liberal Democracy." *The Review of Politics* 59 (1997): 561–92.

Friedman, Edward. "Does China Have the Cultural Preconditions for Democracy?"*Philosophy East and West* 49 (1999): 346–59.

Gregory, John S. *The West and China since 1500.* New York: Palgrave MacMillan, 2003.

Grieder, Jerome B. *Hu Shih and the Chinese Renaissance.* Cambridge, MA: Harvard University Press, 1970.

Hale, Robert Lee. "Notes from John Dewey's Lectures on Moral and Political Philosophy: October 1915–January 1916." In *Research in the History of Economic Thought and Methodology: Lectures by John Dewey,* edited by Warren J. Samuels and Donald F. Koch, 57–115. Greenwich, CT: Jai Press, 1989.

Hall, David L., and Roger T. Ames. *The Democracy of the Dead: Dewey, Confucius and the Hope for Democracy in China.* Chicago: Open Court, 1999.

Hersey, John. *The Call.* New York: Knopf, 1985.

Hood, Steven J. "The Myth of Asian-Style Democracy." *Asian Survey* 38 (1998): 853–66.

Hu, Shih. "John Dewey in China." In *Philosophy and Culture—East and West,* edited by Charles Am Moore, 762–79. Honolulu: University of Hawaii Press, 1962.

Huntington, Samuel P. "Democracy's Third Wave." *Journal of Democracy* 2 (1991): 12–34.

Keenan, Barry. *The Dewey Experiment in China: Educational Reform and Political Power in the Early Republic.* Cambridge, MA: Harvard University Press, 1977.

Keller, Otto. Review of *Letters from China and Japan. St. Louis Post-Dispatch,* 7 August 1920.

Koch, Donald F. "Internal Conflict and the Development of Dewey's Moral, Political and Legal Philosophy." In *Research in the History of Economic Thought and*

Methodology: Lectures by John Dewey, Moral and Political Philosophy, edited by
    Warren J. Samuels and Donald F. Koch. Greenwich, CT: Jai Press, 1989.

Lin, Yu-sheng. *The Crisis of Chinese Consciousness: Radical Antitraditionalism in the
    May Fourth Era.* Madison: University of Wisconsin Press, 1979.

Martin, Jay. *The Education of John Dewey: A Biography.* New York: Columbia Uni-
    versity Press, 2002.

Meisner, Maurice. *Li Ta-Chao and the Origin of Chinese Marxism.* Cambridge, MA:
    Harvard University Press, 1967.

Moorehead, Caroline. *Bertrand Russell: A Life.* New York: Viking, 1992.

Ou, Tsuin-chen. "Dewey's Lectures and Influence in China." In *Guide to the
    Works of John Dewey,* edited by Ann Boydston, 339–62. Carbondale: South-
    ern Illinois University Press, 1970.

P., J. E. Review of *Letters from China and Japan. Pacific Review,* December 1920,
    429–30.

Pepper, Stephen C. Review of *The Public and Its Problems. International Journal of
    Ethics* 38 (1928): 478–80.

Pepper, Suzanne. *Radicalism and Education Reform in 20th Century China.* New
    York: Cambridge University Press, 1996.

Remer, C. F. "John Dewey in China." *Millard's Review* 13 (3 July 1920): 266–68.

———. "John Dewey's Responsibility for American Opinion." *Millard's Review*
    13 (10 July 1920): 321–22.

Review of *Letters from China and Japan. Boston Evening Transcript,* 1 June 1920.

Review of *Letters from China and Japan. New York Tribune,* 16 May 1920.

Review of *Letters from China and Japan. Unity,* 4 November 1920.

Rockefeller, Steven C. *John Dewey: Religious Faith and Democratic Humanism.* New
    York: Columbia University Press, 1991.

Ronald, W. Clark. *The Life of Bertrand Russell.* New York: Knopf, 1976.

Ross, Ralph. Introduction to *The Middle Works of John Dewey.* Vol. 12, *The Collected
    Works of John Dewey, 1882–1953: The Electronic Edition,* edited by Larry A.
    Hickman, ix–xxx. Charlottesville, VA: InteLex, 1996.

Russell, Bertrand. *The Problem of China.* London: Allen and Unwin, 1922.

———. *The Selected Letters of Bertrand Russell: The Public Years, 1914–1970,* edited
    by Nicholas Griffin. London: Routledge, 2001.

Ryan, Alan. *John Dewey and the High Tide of American Liberalism.* New York: Nor-
    ton, 1995.

Schwarcz, Vera. *The Chinese Enlightenment: Intellectuals and the Legacy of the May
    Fourth Movement of 1919.* Berkeley: University of California Press, 1986.

Schwartz, Benjamin I. *Chinese Communism and the Rise of Mao.* Cambridge, MA:
    Harvard University Press, 1951.

Sidorsky, David. Introduction to *The Later Works of John Dewey.* Vol. 3, *The Col-
    lected Works of John Dewey, 1882–1953: The Electronic Edition,* edited by Larry
    A. Hickman, ix–xxxiii. Charlottesville, VA: InteLex, 1996.

Singer, Peter. *One World: The Ethics of Globalization.* New Haven, CT: Yale Uni-
    versity Press, 2002.

Sizer, Nancy F. "John Dewey's Ideas in China, 1919–21." *Comparative Education
    Review* 10 (1966): 390–403.

Spence, Jonathan D. *To Change China: Western Advisers in China, 1620–1960.* New York: Penguin Books, 1980.

———. *The Search for Modern China.* New York: Norton, 1990.

Stevenson, Harold W., and James W. Stigler. *The Learning Gap: Why Our Schools Are Failing and What We Can Learn from Japanese and Chinese Education.* New York: Simon and Schuster, 1992.

Su, Zhixin. "Teaching, Learning and Reflective Acting: A Dewey Experiment in Chinese Teacher Education." *Teachers College Record* 98 (1996): 126–52.

Sun, Youzhong. "John Dewey in China: Yesterday and Today." *Transactions of the Charles S. Pierce Society* 35 (1999): 69–88.

Tan, Sor-hoon. *Confucian Democracy: A Deweyan Reconstruction.* Albany: State University of New York Press, 2003.

———. "China's Pragmatist Experiment in Democracy: Hu Shih's Pragmatism and Dewey's Influence in China." In *The Range of Pragmatism and the Limits of Philosophy,* edited by Richard Shusterman, 43–62. Oxford: Blackwell, 2005.

Tiles, Jim E. "Democracy as Culture." In *Justice and Democracy: Cross-Cultural Perspectives,* edited by Ron Bontekoe and Marietta Stepaniants, 119–31. Honolulu: University of Hawaii Press, 1997.

Tu, Wei-ming. *Confucian Ethics Today: The Singapore Challenge.* Singapore: Curriculum Development Institute of Singapore, 1984.

Utley, Jonathan G. "American Views of China, 1900–1915." In *America Views China: American Images of China Then and Now,* edited by Jonathan Goldstein, Jerry Israel, and Hilary Conroy, 114–31. Bethlehem, PA: Lehigh University Press, 1991.

Westbrook, Robert B. *John Dewey and American Democracy.* Ithaca, NY: Cornell University Press, 1991.

Secondary Sources in Chinese

Boan (柏盦). "The Responses to Dewey from the Educational Circle of Hangzhou" (杭州教育界對杜威的感想). *Academic Lamp* (學燈), 23 June 1920.

Cai, Yuanpei (蔡元培). "A Speech Given at the Dinner Party of Dr. Dewey's Sixtieth Birthday" (在杜威博士60之生日晚餐會上之演說). In *Dewey on China* (杜威談中國), edited by Yihong Shen, 329–30. Hangzhou: Zhejiang Literature and Art, 2001.

Chen, Duxiu (陳獨秀). "The Basis for the Realization of Democracy" (實行民治的基礎). Vol. 2 of *Selected Writings of Chen Duxiu* (陳獨秀著作選), edited by Jianshu Ren, Tongmo Zhang, and Xinzhong Wu, 28–39. Shanghai: Shanghai People's Press, 1993.

———. "What Is New Education?" (新教育是什麼). *A Collection of Educational Essays by Chen Duxiu* (陳獨秀教育論著選), edited by Xiemei Qi and Zhude Shao, 281–90. Beijing: People's Education Press, 1995.

———. "A Letter to Mr. Russell from Duxiu" (獨秀致羅素先生的信). In *Russell on China* (羅素談中國), edited by Yihong Shen, 379. Hangzhou: Zhejiang Literature and Art, 2001.

D., T. "A Critique of Dewey's Lecture" (評杜威底演講). *Awakening* (覺悟), 18 June 1920, Random Thoughts section.

Fei, Juetian (費覺天). "A Critique of Dewey's Social and Political Philosophy" (評杜威底社會與政治哲學). *The Review of Reviews* (評論之評論) 2 (1921): 1–18.

Feng, Chongyi (馮崇義). *Russell and China* (羅素與中國). Beijing: Sanlian Bookstore, 1998.

Fulu (伏廬) [孫伏園]. "Dr. Dewey Is Gone Today" (杜威博士今日去了). *Morning Post* (晨報), 11 July 1921, Miscellaneous Notes section.

———. "Mr. Russell Is also Gone Today" (羅素先生今日也去了). *Morning Post* (晨報), 11 July 1921, Miscellaneous Notes section.

Gao, Juemin (高覺敏). "The Problems of Americanized Education" (囫圇吞棗式的美國化教育). *Journal of Education* (教育雜誌) 17 (1925): 3.

Gu, Hongliang (顧紅亮). *The Misreading of Pragmatism: The Influence of Dewey's Philosophy on Modern Chinese Philosophy* (實用主義的誤讀:杜威哲學對中國現代哲學的影響). Shanghai: East China Normal University Press, 2000.

He, Shaohan (何紹韓). "The So-Called New Education" (余之所謂新教育). *Educational Tide* (教育潮) 1 (1923): 51–52.

Hu, Shih. "More Talk of Problems and Less Talk of Isms" (多談些問題少談些主義). In *Dewey and China* (杜威與中國), edited by Baogui Zhang, 183–87. Shijiazhuang: Hebei People's Press, 2001.

Kui (樾). "Experimentalism and Scientific Life" (實驗主義與科學的生活). *Academic Lamp* (學燈), 15 November 1919.

Li, Jiehua (黎潔華). "A List of Dewey's Activities in China" (杜威在華活動年表). In *Dewey on China* (杜威談中國), edited by Yihong Shen, 369–98. Hangzhou: Zhejiang Literature and Art, 2000.

Liang, Qichao (梁啟超). "Travel Impressions from Europe" (歐遊心影錄). In *A Selection of Essays on the Controversy over Eastern and Western Civilizations before and after May Fourth* (五四前後東西文化問題論戰文選), edited by Song Chen, 349–90. Beijing: Xinhua, 1989.

Liang, Shuming (梁漱溟). *Eastern and Western Cultures and Their Philosophies* (東西文化及其哲學). Taipei: Commercial Press, 2002.

———. *A Final Reflection on the National Salvation Movement in China* (中國民族自救運動之最後覺悟). Taipei: Academic Press, 1971.

———. "Fundamental Ideas in Dewey's Philosophy of Education" (杜威教育哲學之根本概念). In *A Collection of Educational Essays by Liang Shuming* (梁漱溟教育論著選), edited by Qiufan Ma, 119–34. Beijing: People's Education Press, 1994.

Lin, Zhaoyin (林昭音). "A Few Questions about Dewey's *Democracy and Education*" (讀杜威平民主義與教育之幾個疑問). *The Chinese Educational Circles* (中華教育界) 12 (1923): 1–6.

Liu, Haifeng (劉海峰). *Educational Angles of Civil Service Examinations* (科舉考試的教育視角). Wuhan: Hubei Education Press,1995.

Mei, Guangdi (梅光迪). *Writings of Professor K. T. Mei* (梅光迪文錄). Taipei: Chinese Library, 1968.

Mo, Fenglin(繆鳳林). "A Review of Dewey's *Democracy and Education*" (評杜威平民與教育). *Critical Review* (學衡) 10 (1922): 1–12.

Qu, Qiubai (瞿秋白). "Pragmatism and Revolutionary Philosophy" (實驗主義與革命哲學). In *Selected Writings of Qu Qiubai* (瞿秋白選集). Beijing: People's Press, 1985.

"Report from the Farewell Banquet for Dewey" (五團體恭踐杜威之言論). *Morning Post* (晨報), 26 May 1921, sec. 3.

Russell, Bertrand. "The Bolsheviks and World Politics" (布爾什維克與世界政治). In *Russell on China* (羅素談中國), edited by Yihong Shen, 309–14. Hangzhou: Zhejiang Literature and Art, 2001.

———. "Bolshevik Thoughts" (布爾什維克的思想). In *Russell on China*, edited by Yihong Shen, 315–20.

———. "China's Road to Freedom" (中國的到自由之路). In *Russell on China*, edited by Yihong Shen, 321–30.

Shen, Yihong (沈益洪), ed. *Russell on China* (羅素談中國). Hangzhou: Zhejiang Literature and Art, 2001.

Shoying (瘦影). "The Real Meaning of Pragmatism Is Not Copying-with-the-Environment-Ism'" (實驗主義的真義絕不是對付環境主義). *Beijing University Student Weekly* (北京大學學生週刊) 13 (28 March 1920).

Wang, Mouzu(汪懋祖). "The Problems of Education at the Present Time and Their Remedies" (現時我國教育上之弊病與其救治方略). *Critical Review* (學衡), 22 (1923): 1–5.

Wu, Jiangling (吳江玲). "A Critique of Dewey's Philosophy of Education" (評杜威之教育哲學). *Academic Lamp* (學燈), 22 October 1922.

Xiping (希平). "My Response to Dewey's Experimentalism" (我對杜威試驗主義的感想). *Awakening* (覺悟), 27 July 1920, Commentary section.

Zhang, Baoqui (張寶貴), ed. *Dewey and China* (杜威與中國). Shijiazhuang: Hebei People's Press, 2001.

Zhenying (震瀛), "My Hope for Bertrand Russell" (我對羅素的希望). *Awakening* (覺悟), 15 October 1920, Commentary section.

Zhixi (志希) [羅家倫]. "Dr. Dewey's School and Society" (杜威博士的學校與社會). *Renaissance* (新潮) 2 (1919): 187–91.

———. "Dr. Dewey's 'Moral Principles in Education'" (杜威博士的德育原理). *Renaissance* (新潮) 2 (1919): 192–95.

Zhu, Jin (朱進). "Why Are Scholars Revered by the World?" (學者何以為世人所崇拜). *New Education* (新教育) 1 (1919): 361–64.

Zhu, Qianzhi (朱謙之). "A Manifesto against Examinations" (反抗考試的宣言). *Beijing University Student Weekly* (北京大學學生週刊) 13 (28 March 1920).

INDEX

❖

Addams, Jane, 31, 84
"America and the Far East," 73
Ames, Roger T., 117, 118, 119, 120
anarchism, 28, 46, 68
Art as Experience, 114, 122
"As the Chinese Think," 62, 80, 81
Asia, 8, 80, 85
Awakening (Chinese periodical), 44, 45

Babbitt, Irving, 33, 54, 55. *See also* Mei
   Guangdi
Barnes, Alert C., 4, 51, 79
Bergson, Henri, 23, 53, 127n28
Boan, 44
"Bolsheviks and World Politics" (Rus-
   sell), 27
Bolshevism (bolshevik), 24, 41, 46, 47,
   49; Dewey on, 50; Russell on, 27–29
Bourne, Randolph S., 61, 84
Boxer Uprising, 2
Bullert, Gary, 89

Cai Yuanpei, 14
Characters and Events, 80
Chen Duxiu, 14, 36, 63; initial interest
   in Dewey, 47–48; letter to Russell, 27;
   on new education, 60
"China's Road to Freedom" (Russell),
   27–29
"Chinese National Sentiment," 98
"Chinese Philosophy of Life," 62, 80
Chow, Tse-tsung, 32, 48, 50, 135n15
Clopton, Robert W., 5, 126n18, 129n56
Communism, Chinese: Dewey, com-
   ment on, 50; founding of party, 27,
   41; government, purging of prag-
   matism, 9, 36, 41; Russian influences
   on, 47

Confucian democracy, 11, 115–17, 120
Confucianism: Confucius, relations
   with Dewey, 7, 11, 14, 26; Liang
   Shuming, in defense of, 54, 123; ;
   Russell on, 14; under attack during
   May Fourth, 8, 14, 53
"Creative Democracy—The Task be-
   fore Us," 113
Critical Review (Chinese periodical), 54
cultural reformism, of Hu Shih, 30, 35,
   36, 37

Dalton Plan, 56
Daoism, 14, 80
Darwinism, 15
Democracy and Education, 13, 54, 55, 60,
   105, 107, 113, 114, 123
Dewey, Alice Chipman, 3, 34, 66, 67,
   69, 134n9
Dewey, Jane, 85
Dewey, John: on Chinese philosophy of life, 62, 80–81; on Chinese
   revolutionary idealism, 50–51; on
   Chinese social psychology, 77; in
   comparison with Russell, 26–29;
   decision to visit China, 3–4; on
   democracy as a way of life, 113–15;
   "Dewey experiment in China,"
   6, 10, 35, 62–63; on differences
   between Japan and China, 4; differences with Hu Shih, 35, 38, 39,
   65, 67, 83; on Eurocentrism, 75;
   farewell banquet for, 29; on hands-
   off policy, 72–73; on Hegel's theory
   of state, 93–94; on his own influence in China, 6, 39; on interest and
   discipline, 57–59; on internation-
   ism, 87–92, 124; on Marxism, 19,

149